ESPIONAGE, STATECRAFT, AND THE THEORY OF REPORTING

ESPIONAGE, STATECRAFT, AND THE THEORY OF REPORTING

A PHILOSOPHICAL ESSAY ON INTELLIGENCE MANAGEMENT

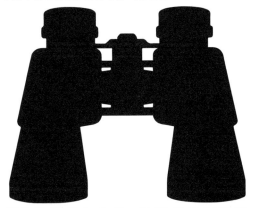

NICHOLAS RESCHER

UNIVERSITY OF PITTSBURGH PRESS

Published by the University of Pittsburgh Press, Pittsburgh, Pa., 15260
Copyright © 2018, University of Pittsburgh Press
Manufactured in the United States of America
Printed on acid-free paper
10 9 8 7 6 5 4 3 2 1

Cataloging-in-Publication data is available from the Library of Congress

ISBN 13: 978–0-8229–4473–7
ISBN 10: 0–8229–4473–1

Cover art: Shutterstock, iStock, and 123RF.com.
Cover design by Bruce Gore

CONTENTS

PREFACE

WE HUMANS ARE *HOMO SAPIENS*: knowledge is the compass by which we navigate our way in the world. And all of the issues of information management in the context of reports—acquisition, formulation, recording and recovery, transmission, translation—are crucial factors in cognitive theory. And they all play an important and characteristic role in matters of military and diplomatic intelligence.

Intelligent human interaction is impossible without report-transmitted information about the interpreter. Action and reaction in these matters is unavoidable. And the complexity to which it gives rise poses never-ending challenges in a way that makes the study of intelligence management at once challenging in its complexity and interesting in its impact on human affairs.

My brief involvement with military intelligence occurred when I served in the United States Marine Corps during the Korean War. When I entered the Marine Corps in 1952, I was assigned to intelligence and given the corresponding specialist classification 0300. But it soon transpired that I was needed elsewhere, and I spent the rest of my service stationed at the Marie Barracks in Washington, DC, as a mathematics instructor at the Marine Corps Institute's correspondence school. In the end, my interest in intelligence developed in a personal rather than professional capacity.

This book is greatly indebted to the excellent support I have received in the course of manuscript preparation from Estelle Burris, my invaluable assistant of many years standing.

ESPIONAGE, STATECRAFT, AND THE THEORY OF REPORTING

INTRODUCTION

LIFE BEING WHAT IT IS, situations of competition and conflict are unavoidable among and even within human communities. And the rational management of conflicts is impossible in the absence of information about the capabilities and intentions of one's opponents. Obtaining reports of such matters becomes an indispensable goal. The very structure of organizations is defined by arrangements for who reports to whom.

The mythological patron of reporting is Mercury, the messenger of the gods, and the value of reporting has been acknowledged throughout history. Short of conversation, there is no form of human communication more extensive and prominent than reportage. Reports of one sort or another use our prime instruments for informed thinking, seeing that virtually the whole of what we know about what goes on in the world comes to us through reports. The topic of reporting has various philosophical dimensions: logical, epistemic, ethical, practical, and others. However, the present deliberations will focus on the epistemic dimension and will seek to integrate the rational theory of reporting into the wider setting of knowledge-related issues. The complexity of the overall problem-area is immense, and it is judicious to transit its components one at a time.

There are innumerably different type of reports: articles in newspapers, encyclopedias, reference books, accounts of travel writers, police reports, and on and on. In the present discussion, however, illustrations will be mainly developed with a view to the reports of diplomats and espionage agents. For the features of reports in general stand out with particular vividness here. Accordingly, the present book is emphatically not an essay on journalism but focuses predominantly on issues of diplomatic and military intelligence. It is predicated in the idea that the tradecraft of reporting in the context of intelligence operations opens an inductive window upon the epistemology of reportage.

While philosophers since Descartes have hankered for absolute certainty, this is simply unrealistic. What actually passes for knowledge among us in everyday life is information that enjoys reasonable assurance even if not categorical certainty. And most of this comes to us through reports of various kinds. Accordingly, the epistemology of reporting is—and should be—of paramount concern for us. To be sure, the philosophical skeptic, inclined to think that we really cannot know anything with adequate assurance, would propose to see all reports as functioning on the level playing field of undifferentiated unacceptability. As skeptics have generally themselves admitted, such a position can of course find no traction in the practical realm of human affairs and action—for obvious reasons. Most of what we take ourselves to know is not something certifiable with the Cartesian certainty of "clear and distinct knowledge" but rather something possessed of suboptimal credibility and reliability. Our knowledge, like our domestic domicile, is built for use in standard and normal conditions: it is not an impregnable fortress. And reporting constitutes a prime sector of knowledge management.

Reports crowd upon us at every turn—via the media, in work situations, and even in casual conversation. Only some of the time do they really matter in their bearing on what we should be doing in the management of our affairs. But it is bound to happen, sufficiently often, that a clear understanding of the issues involved with reportage serves a constructive function, especially in the crucial area of "matters of state."

It is not the aim of this book to engage with the technical issues of intelligence management—nor, for that matter, with the vast technical issues of information science, communication theory, testimony, and related formal disciplines. Rather its concern is with the most basic and fundamental issues of reporting practice—with special emphasis on matters of stats relating to statecraft and international and military affairs. Accordingly, the range of examples focus upon natural security reportage of the sort provided to a government by its diplomatic and intelligence reporting agents with a view to the management of matters of state. This is done not because it is typical of reporting—there is perhaps no such thing as "typical reportage"—but rather because the sorts of issues that arise with reporting in support of statecraft here occur with particular prominence. And so the reports that will primarily concern us here are those that address issues of intended conflict in warfare and diplomacy—the reports of diplomatic and espionage agents. After all, intelligence information in matters of statecraft and of warfare, that "continuation of politics by other means," afford the most vivid examples of need for and use of reports. Accordingly, the illustrative example to be given here will be drawn from this domain—primarily in the context of the vast mega-conflict of the Second World War.

The introduction of precision and clarity into deliberations about reporting is a much needed desideratum, and the present book will undertake some steps in this direction. The absence of a general introduction to the theory of reporting is regrettable, and it is the author's hope that his book will make a small contribution toward filling a regrettably regrettable gap.

The overall plan of the book stands as follows: It begins with an initial stage setting of the reporting process that locates it within the overall project of information management, to which we stand committed in the natural order of things. It then proceeds chapter by chapter to examine the principle components of reporting: the basic sources, the contribution of intent, the transmission of the message, and then matters of interpretation, evaluating, and utilization. The aim is to provide, step by step, a critical survey of the prospects and problems that characterize information reportage in intelligence matters.

A clear lesson to emerge from these deliberations is the convoluted complexity of intelligence report management. So many different and often conflicting considerations are in play here that the surprise is not that the business can be managed well but that it can be managed at all.

Finally, a brief terminological clarification. As here used, the verb "to report" indicates the act, and "a report" is the result of its exercise; "reporting" is the activity at issue with the act, and "reportage" will be used both for the collective product of the activity when engaged in repeatedly and also for the reporting practice at large.

CHAPTER 1

REPORTS AND OUR NEED FOR INFORMATION

THE MANY-FACETED NATURE OF REPORTS

Even in classical antiquity, reporting by observers, spies, and information agents regarding potential enemies—and friends—was a common practice.[1] And we nowadays live in what has become known as "the information age." As the volume of reporting grows, it eventually reaches virtually unmanageable proportions. We even need reports to find our way through the lush jungle of reporting—reference aides of all sorts: indices, handbooks, bibliographies, search engines.

Information by its nature is a matter of fact (or purported fact) about how matters stand in an area of concern, actual or potential. And the principal function of a report is to convey useful information about a certain factual issue. There is only so much information that people can acquire on their own: for the most part they are dependent on the reportings of others. People crave informative reporting. They eagerly await the delivery of newspapers and the airing of newscasts; they subscribe to newsletters; they surf the Internet. The arrival of reports can constitute pivotal episodes in people's lives. American adults of the day are likely to recall, even down to minute details about what they were doing and thinking, when reports first reached them regarding the surrender of Germany in the Second World War, the atomic bombing of Hiroshima, the assassination of President Kennedy, or the terror attacks of 9/11. Yet while reports generally exist to provide information, this is not always and invariably so. After all, newspaper reportage functions not only to provide information but also to provide entertainment as well—as with per the reporting of "human interest" stories.

The term "report" is rather flexible. It can stand literally for the text conveyed or for the information conveyed in that text. When an agent reports "Three missiles were fired but only one hit the target," one would not hesitate to say that he reported that two missiles missed the target. There is also a range of other borderline cases. For example, is an English translation of *War and Peace* a version of the book itself or is it the translator's report that "If Tolstoy had written his book in English he would have written something like this . . . "?

Reports have an impact on the information already at our disposal—what we take ourselves to know. This impact can take many forms:

- It can be *ampliative* and supplement the information we have.
- It can be *negatively corrective*, indicating that what we presumably accept is incorrect.
- It can be *positively corrective,* replacing what we previously accepted by something else.

All of these modes of reportage are—or should be—welcome. All of them improve our cognitive position. To be sure, negatively corrective reports are somewhat frustrating: we thought we had an answer where we now simply have a blank, but of course ignorance is generally preferable to error.

The significance of reports varies enormously. Many are trivial and routine, addressing such issues as weather, traffic congestion, crime, or stock exchange transactions. Other reports communicate cataclysmic news items, such as Japan's attack on Pearl Harbor or the United States' atomic bombing of Hiroshima. Some reportage opens new worlds to view, as per the travel reports of Marco Polo. Then too there is the manifold of so-called announcements, ranging from things for sale and opportunities for employment to weddings, births, and funerals. It is reasonable to regard even interrogations and imperatives as conveying reports. Thus, asking "How much is 2 plus 2?" would seem to convey "The questioner requests that you to answer how much 2 plus 2 is." And again the injunction "Come here" could be reconsidered as simply "The questioner requests that you come to him or her."

One particularly significant mode of reportage is the projection of for-the-record reports of official bodies: the deliberations and decisions of legislative or regulatory bodies or legal proceedings, the "acts" of learned societies or investigative bodies and the like. Scholarly and scientific papers report the findings of investigations to the wider community of fellow specialists. Then too there are the for-the-record reports of fact recording proceedings: tax rolls, census reports, deed records, patient registries, estate inventories, or—much earlier—the Domesday Book. Since the invention of bureaucracies in Mesopotamia, record keeping has been an ongoing venture in creating reports.

Defective information is the bane of reporting. Good reporting should augment relevant knowledge, but knowledge unfortunately admits of innumerable defects: ignorance, error, inaccuracy, ill-grounding, distortion (bias, mis-emphasis), and others. Whatever question we may have in view—be it oriented to what, where, when, why, how, and so on—can be answered imperfectly. Adequate reporting should be correct, accurate, credible, and relevant to the reportee's concern, all of which is easier said than done.

Reporting is thus an almost endlessly many-faceted process whose range knows no limits: weather reports, stock market reports, news reports (even "news flashes"), obituaries, wedding announcements, police blotters—the list is potentially interminable. Nowadays accidents of all sorts engender reports. Be they auto accidents, train accidents, airplane accidents, mine accidents, industrial accidents, or whatever, there is invariably investigation by relevant authorities to examine and report upon the circumstances of their causation. Predictions constitute yet another important category of reports: weather forecasts, economic forecasts, traffic forecasts, and the like all afford needed information. Such reports are indispensable tools for conforming present action to plans and policies for the longer term.

The message of a report is its declarative substance—the body of information that it conveys. Reports encompass the whole range from single lines ("Air raid: Pearl Harbor. This is no drill.") to massively tome-like proportions. Some reports are even large multivolume ventures. This is particularly true of the investigative reports that ensue on major disasters of some sort—the Pearl Harbor commissioner's report, the 9/11 Commission Report, the Three-Mile Island incident report, the Challenger disaster report. Such reports are complex in every applicable dimension—source, substance, and audience alike—they are, in effect, report conglomerates that comprise a mass of constituent subreports.

How long and comprehensive should reports be? In theory, report lengths cover a great range: words, sentences, paragraphs, chapters, books, book series. There are micro-reports and macro-reports. Even single words can convey a report—for example, "Fire." And then there are the multivolume reports of inquiry commissions such as those addressing the Pearl Harbor attack or the Three Mile Island meltdown. The work of these macro-reports is not only to present information but also—and more pivotally—to provide context through providing a framework for interpreting otherwise available resources.

Reports should, of course, be truthful. But the conception of "the actual truth" is something of an idealization. What we actually have to deal with in life is "our putative truth"—the truth as we see it, comprising all of those claims that we deem ourselves entitled to accept as true. And it is just here that problems arise because we may well (flawed beings that we are) deem it sensible to accept in one context something we are reluctant to accept (or even inclined to reject) in another. This issue comes to the fore in situations where the endorsement of claims becomes differentiated in the light of different standards of acceptance. In the face of potential conflicts, are we to accept the report that

- comes from the most reliable source
- best represents the consensus of varying numerous sources
- fits best into the framework of pre-existing information
- offers the best prospect of successful instrumentation
- is the most promising in misfortune-avoidance in the wake of implementation?

There is of course no assurance of uniformity among these different standards: they are to pull us in different directions. And in resolving such problems, the attitude toward risk of error is bound to play a pivotal role.

Most reports are commonplace. There are also some rather eccentric and extraordinary modes of reporting. One instance is the reporting of religious visions of the sort examined in William James's *Varieties of Religious Experience*. Another is the reportage of relativity induced by drugs or nonstandard physical conditions such as long-term evolution. Here the source and the reporter are one and the same, and the subject of reportage is the experience of the reporter rather than occurrences in "the external world." The epistemology of the matter differs with the sort of information at issue here and serves to put this sort of subjectively experiential reporting outside the range of our present concerns. UFO sightings, though a distinctive mode of reportage, will also be put aside here.

In military usage, to report is often simply to indicate one's presence by "showing up." And someone about whom people speaks favorably is said to be "of good report." Personal activity reports are a prominent feature of the police state. In such a system, Big Brother may or may not actually be watching you but Nosy Neighbor will almost certainly be filing reports on you with the Stasi-like "state security" apparatus. Such reporting becomes a crucial resource for social control in dictatorially managed societies. When a soldier is placed "on report," it means that a higher authority is being called upon to deal with some misdeed of the soldier.

Reportage is fraught with issues of decision. The reporter has to decide what to report, how to formulate it, how and to whom to transmit it. The recipient of the report, or reportee, has to decide whether or not to accept the report at face value, how to interpret it, and what to do about it. There is virtually no limit to the possible functions of reports: not only to inform but also to direct, to counsel, to recommend, and even on occasion to annoy. Of course whatever can be used can also be abused. Reports can convey misinformation as well as information. It is little wonder that contract bridge was the most favored game among intelligence operators in the Second World War. For, in the process of bidding that precedes the play of the cards, every step taken by every party in this game of team conflict is either a report on the content of one's card holdings or a specific request for information about one's partner's hand. One of the key lessons that is immediately brought home in this context is that miscommunication and failure to make proper use of reported information can be fatal to one's cause.

There is, regrettably, such a thing as malreporting. Leaks of unfavorable and discrediting information, "character assassinations," malign insinuations, disinformation, "false news," and the like all represent a category of attack reports. In dictatorships and democratic societies alike, stressed and even faked reports are favored weapons in hate campaigns for political manipulation. This sort of disinformation constitutes the dark side of reportage. A passport is a report of sorts on the person who is its bearer, yet here a forged document represents a foray into disinformation. Like many other forms of false reportage—in income tax matters, for example—those who are in violation run afoul not just of propriety but of the law.

Whistle-blowing is perhaps the most dramatic mode of reporting in the context of organizations at large. The aim of the enterprise is exposure—be it of incompetence, law breaking, regulatory violation, or some other sort of malfeasance. Here the reporter is entirely self-selected and self-motivated. And the recipient of the report is rather open-ended—perhaps a regulatory agency or perhaps the world at large through the mediation of a journalist. The reporter's motivation to report can be very diversified—possibly financial, possibly for retribution or revenge, possibly in the interest of the public. In any event, whistle-blowing reportage amounts to a complex cry of alarm. As such, it does well to be loud, clear, and seemingly well intentioned.

As Clausewitz already noted long ago, in conflict situations the advantage generally lies with the attacker. And it does so in several key regards. For the attacker has a *physical* advantage in being able to select the time and place of the initial assault, adjusting both of them to capitalize on the opponent's weakness. Moreover, the attacker has the *psychological* advantage of realizing exactly what is happening as regards the why, what, and how of it. And additionally the attacker has an *intelligence* advantage as well, in view of the fact that for offense one needs information about the opponent's vulnerabilities, while for defense one needs information about the opponent's intentions. And there is a tremendous disparity, seeing that vulnerabilities are generally open to inspection, while intentions generally are not.

RECIPIENTS AND REPORTEES

To deal productively with a vast mass of information, great care must be taken to delimit precisely the questions one is intending to resolve. For unless those questions are narrowly targeted and issue well delimited, the amorphous mass of information continues to be intractable. It does not help much that the individual one is looking for is listed somewhere in the Manhattan telephone directory, but if one is asking for a Tom Thomason, one has a better chance of putting that body of information to productive use. Context-based interpretation is not just important for the effective use of reported material, it is also a requisite in forming the questions that this material is intended to address. A reportee who gives his or her reporters a clear picture of their desiderata is in a better position to make good use of them. In matters of intelligence the question-answer relation stands in symbolic coordination. Just this gave Tokyo's request for details of ship location in Pearl Harbor the potential for substantial significance.

A report should of course deal with matters that will interest its recipient. Prominent here is information regarding one's competitors—especially rivals, opponents, and enemies. One wants to know especially about their resources, their activities, their capabilities, and their plans and intentions. On such matters one is likely to make worst-case assumptions, so it is useful here to replace mere conjecture by factual reality.

In conflict situations all sources of information are welcome, not just those reporting on one's enemies but also those reporting on one's allies as well. (One never knows: In the Second World War, Joseph Stalin constantly worried that Britain and America might seek a separate peace with Germany. Inversely, the Anglophone powers suspected that Stalin himself might do so, with each side taking a strong interest in the invisible intentions of its allies.[2])

Reports present facts—or at least purport to do so. Works of avowed fiction cannot be characterized as reports. Deliberately fictitious reports are in effect forgeries. Reports thus convey information, and this process has four main components: *realization*, its *emission*, its *transmission*, and its *reception*. There will be some originator who obtains the reported information and then does the reporting, a process of mediating transmission, and some intended recipient who receives the report and may or may not accept what it claims, seeing it as information or misinformation, respectively.

Reporting is information transfer from a *reporter* to a recipient *reportee*. Reporters who want their reports to be taken seriously do well to foster a reputation for accurate reporting, and providing credible reports is the best way to move in this direction.

The information provided by a reporter in their report to a reportee originates from *sources*. And like a structure, a report is no firmer than its foundation. Ideally, the reportee will be provided by the reporter with enough data so that assurances on this score can be had. Otherwise one gropes about in the situations of he said, she said uncertainty familiar from the law courts. Reports emanating from untrustworthy sources are virtually useless.[3]

Accordingly, the reporting process always involves multiple roles. In particular there will be: suppliers, sources, coordinators, reporters (report transmitter); messages (the reports themselves), and consumers (the recipients and implementers of reports). Of course one and the same individual can play several roles. For example, a news reporter can be the source, coordinator, sender, and even consuming user of one selfsame report.

A reportee is the agent or agency that, by the reporter's intention, is to receive the report. However, the recipient of a report may certainly differ from what the sender intends, so that there is a critical potential difference between the intended reportees and the actual recipients of a report. The reporter himself is sometimes the reportee, as when a report is written for oneself—as an aide-mémoire or a reminder or a statement of record.

A reporter generally does not tell the whole of the story in a single report. Usually there are follow-ups to fill in detail and develop a fuller account—frequently in response to reportee requests. The process of reporting can thus get to be a process of reciprocal and, as it were, dialogical interaction between reporter and reportee, with the occasional role reversal between these parties.

Some reports are made at the initiative of the reporter, others at the initiative of the reportee. Thus expert reports are often commissioned to review processes and procedures. When he suspected that Germany's naval cipher for submarine monitoring might be broken in 1943, Admiral Karl Dönitz commissioned a technical report on its security. His cryptographic experts reported that it was effectively impossible to break the cipher short of making "an industrial scale project" of the effort. Little did contemporary Germans suspect that this is exactly what the British were doing at Bletchley Park, the codebreaking center with its staff of well over 10,000, which was Britain's equivalent of the Manhattan project.[4]

The recipients of reports may be either intended by the reporters in specifically targeting a particular individual or group, or they may be open-ended, with the report accessible to the public at large. And of course reports destined for particular recipients may also be accessed by others—benignly or maliciously. For not only do reports have intended recipients, but they can also have quasi-intended recipients—in particular in matters of espionage or military intelligence, when the sender believes the enemy to be "listening in" on communication. Reports may then convey what is not actually information for its intended recipients but rather misinformation aimed at that illicit recipient.[5]

ISSUES OF REPORT ACCEPTANCE

In accepting reports at face value, the reportee always runs some risk of error. Accordingly, the use that we envision for the reported information becomes a crucial consideration. When large issues are at stake and substantial risks attach to implementing this information, the admonition "Proceed with care!" becomes operative. When the stake is large in that information acceptance carries potential hazards in its wake, one does well to raise the bar of acceptability for reports.

An aura of insecurity generally hoovers about he said, she said reporting. Hearsay reporting has an indirectness that countervails against immediacy and compromises authenticity. The stronger the credentials of a report, the more likely it is to be accepted.

The need for action and its inherent risks exert opposing influences upon the issues of how high the bar for the acceptance of a report gets to be set. Here, as elsewhere, one wants to be especially continuous when the risks are substantial.

Whatever its other merits, a report does nothing for a recipient who does not understand it. This imposes a two-sided burden. The reporter must make the effort to be understandable, and the reportee must develop the necessary smarts to know what he or she is dealing with.

There is a good deal to be said in favor of making reports in writing. This can avert doubts regarding what it is that is being reported and can prevent matters from decaying into hearsay and speculation. At the outset of the Second World War, Winston Churchill gave the following instruction to his war cabinet secretariat: "Let it be clearly understood that all directions emitting from me are made in writing, or should be immediately afterwards confirmed in writing, and that I do not accept any responsibility for matters relating to national defense on which I am alleged to have given decisions unless they are recorded in writing."[6] Administrations all too rarely follow this excellent practice of reporting their wishes and decisions with literal explicitness so as to leave minimal room for misunderstandings and confusion.

Reporting about reports raises complex issues. Thus, in situations of conflict, if A reports to B that C has reported something to D, then B may not have a clue about the context of C's report but may nevertheless lose trust in C simply because of C's contact with D. Knowledge about reporting can convey significant information even when the content of those reports is itself totally unknown.

In general, the best determiners of the adequacy of reports are the recipient reportees whose needs and goals are, after all, the ultimate pivot of the enterprise. Sometimes it is merely information being sought for its own sake; at other times information is needed for the guidance of action. But the merit of a report ultimately pivots on its ability to meet the reportee's needs, whether theoretical or practical. In reporting, as in the retail industry, the consumer's interests are paramount.

This fundamental fact is strikingly manifest in the field of intelligence, especially as it relates to warfare and diplomacy. All of those elaborate efforts to transmit one's opponent's doings are ultimately pointless when the mass of reports that they generate is not effectively exploited to strengthening one's position and improving one's operations on the battlefield or at the negotiating table. As one knowledgeable commentator has observed, "Intelligence must always be relevant to real political or military purposes . . . and it must always be verifiable—for if it is not verifiable, it is, in the strictest sense of the word, worthless: it cannot be believed or used."[7]

REPORT VULNERABILITIES

Given that the function of reports is to convey information, there are two prime categories of report virtues, with one category relating to the information itself (its accuracy, clarity, detail, range, relevance, etc.) and the other to its transmission (faithfulness, timeliness, etc.).

Correspondingly, a wide spectrum of potential weaknesses and errors afflict the reportorial process. The effective utilization of reports requires the due coordination of a great many factors. (The machinery of reporting has many moving parts, all of which must function properly to issue in the effective utilization of reports.) In the end, any source or group of sources can always prove to be incomplete. Notwithstanding the massive monitoring of German radio communications in the Second World War, the Allies never accessed various key items regarding German plans and programs.[8] Reporters find it easier to get at people's declarations than at their thoughts and interactions.

Reports are fragile and vulnerable things whose value is readily compromised in many ways. And the several vulnerabilities of reportage relate to some sort of failure to achieve the objects of the communicative enterprise. There can arise from failings in relation to the organization, transmission, and reception of reportage as per table 1.

To undermine the credibility of a report, one need not proceed by attacking it directly: indirect means can be highly effective. For the large context of relevant background information into which it falls constitutes a crucial factor in assessing the acceptably of reported information. And manipulating this suitably is a major means for undermining the credibility of reports.

In many contexts of reportage, the maintenance of confidentiality is of the essence. In such situations reports are intended—for good

TABLE 1. REPORTING MALFUNCTIONS

I. *Source Failings*
- Inaccurate data: data that are incorrect, imprecise, equivocal, etc.

II. *Reporter Failings*
- incomplete or defective knowledge
- misinformation by failure of due diligence
- dishonesty and deceitful intent
- risking confidentiality and source protection (where needed)

III. *Transmission Failings*
- defective operation and malfunction
- delay and tardiness
- corrupting interference
- compromising secrecy

IV. *Recipient Failings*
- prejudice, prejudgments, or close-mindedness
- incomprehension: inability to grasp the message

---

reason—to reach only certain very particular recipients. In all situations of relevancy and conflict, one's proceedings and plans—and above all one's vulnerabilities—are not matters one would welcome being reported to the opposition.

When the Allies were laying the groundwork for the Normandy invasion in the Second World War, they went to great lengths to signal a crossing in the seemingly more convenient Pas-de-Calais area. The unavoidable occasional signal toward Normandy thus fell into a background context favoring a different alternative—a circumstance that made it tempting to see such reports as mis- or disinformation.

The Allied war plans carried by "the man who never was"—the British officer whose body washed up on a Spanish shore after a presumed airplane accident—were soon reported to the German military, where they reinforced the idea that the Allied cross-channel invasion would come across the Pas-de-Calais and not in Normandy.[9]

It may of course turn out—by accident as it were—that even a false report turns out to be useful to its recipient—accidentally, as it were. The false reports of a Vietnamese attack on the U.S. destroyers Maddox and Turner Joy in the Gulf of Tonkin in August 1964 modified U.S. opinion against the Hanoi regime and led Congress to pass (virtually unopposed) the so-called Gulf of Tokin Resolution, which outlined the use of military force in Southeast Asia. It then proved to be of great aid in enabling the Johnson administration to pursue its aims in the Vietnam War.

THE PRAGMATIC DIMENSION

While reportage has its risks, the fact remains that a fundamental principle of practical reasoning is inherent in the realistic principle that *one has to make do with the best one can manage in the circumstances.* This is clearly not a factual truth. It is, rather, a practical principle of procedure, akin in this respect to a thesis like, "People are always to be trusted until and unless something arises to call their credibility into question." This general principle holds with reports as well.

It should be stressed, however, that the validation of such a practical principle of procedure does not call for establishing its truth. It is, rather, a matter of realizing that by proceeding on its basis we can most effectively and efficiently achieve our relevant objectives. Justification accordingly proceeds ultimately with respect to considerations not so much of truth but of utility.

Reports are cognitive instruments. And the natural mode of assessment of anything instrumental must proceed in terms of its effectiveness and efficiency in its mission and purpose. As the preceding deliberations indicate, there exists a whole host of principles and practices of good reporting. And throughout their nature is indicated by the aims and objectives of the enterprise. For reportage is ultimately a practical and goal-oriented resource, a tool or instrument for the achievement of certain ends. Given this instrumentality, reportage is something that can be done well or poorly. And because, like other instruments, it is of itself ethically neutral, it can be used for ends that are either good or evil.

Like so much else we do, reporting has an ethical dimension: it can be either honest or dishonest. Thus, reportage in conflict situations virtually demands manipulation by managing information favorably—and the opponent's unfavorably—by propaganda. And in addition to the cognitive aspects of reporting is the ethical dimension of the matter. There is no question that lying, deception, deliberate distortion, and the like are reprehensible practices. The rational management of affairs becomes near impossible where one cannot operate on the presumption that reports report the truth—or at any rate the truth as the reporter sees it. And it is this highly cost-effective presumption that anchors the epistemic bearing of the matter. In its absence we could become embarked on an unending regress of checking out the checkers.

To receive a report is one thing; to accept it is another. Only under duly benign conditions will the recipient take a report's message at face value by accepting it as fact. Certain conditions are critical prerequisites here—in particular, source trustworthiness, transmission reliability, and content plausibility. Let us consider them in turn.

CHAPTER 2

REPORTING AND ITS SOURCES

SOURCE ISSUES

For maximal efficiency, reports should put first things first. In a given (hypothetical) situation a report may present the following facts:

- Someone died at sea.
- The deceased was a male in is fifties.
- He died in the early morning hours.
- He had watched television the preceding evening.
- He wore a nautical jacket.
- He was the president of the United States.

But this sort of presentation just will not do. Sensible reporting puts first things first, placing the information that is of superior importance and/or interest up front. Novelists and other writers of fiction can reverse this policy to build up suspense, but such enterprises are different in nature, as they aim to entertain and intrigue. With effective reporting, appropriate prioritization is a prime consideration.

Some reporting is done in line with general instructions of procedure, some in response to specific requests, and some is automatic and ongoing, as per the location reports of vehicle GPS systems. To serve its informative function, a report must not merely be true but also credible. And the credibility of reports turns principally on two factors: the reliability of their source and the plausibility of their content. A report can serve its informative mission only when the recipient has good reason for regarding its information as true. And such reliability is a matter of reliable is as reliable does. It is manifested through performance—through accumulating a good track record.

A report is *rejected* when the recipient endorses its denial; it is *declined* when the recipient suspends judgment regarding its affirmation. This important distinction is often insufficiently heeded in the epistemology of information processing. For in line with its distinction, there are two very different reactions to the reliability of sources. They can be deemed untrustworthy, in the sense that one systemically declines to accept their claims and suspends judgment about them, or they can be deemed deceptive, in that one inclines to reject their reports and accept the contrary of what they claim. In the former case we treat our sources with unbelief, in the latter with disbelief. When we have lost confidence in the competence of a source, we refrain from accepting its reports. When we actually distrust the source—when we think it has become corrupted or even "turned"—then we will outright disbelieve its claims. (Note that the second situation is actually more informative: It obliquely provides us with information in hand, whereas the former leaves a blank. Being reported to by a deceptive source affects our judgment of the *probability* of the truth of what is reported, by way of decreasing it.)

When should we accept a claim to supposed fact and add it to the stock of our beliefs—our putative knowledge? This is obviously a question that engages both the philosopher and the ordinary man. Philosophers incline to rely on Bishop Butler's idea that probability is the guide of life. Probability, in the sense of harmonization with the body of already available knowledge, is seen as the pivot. Accordingly, these theorists base their proceeding on the substantiating evidence that speaks for the substantive content of a claim.

If a source is to supply useful information, then this source must have three key characteristics. First, the source must be *knowledgeable:* their information on the matter at issue must be pertinent, correct, and accurate. Second, the source must be *candid:* he or she must be prepared to transmit the information they actually have in a comprehensive and accurate way, avoiding errors of omission and commission. And third, the source must be *accessible* through employing a channel of transmission that appropriately conveys their reports. Unfortunately, every aspect of reporting is liable to error. The reporter can be misinformed. The reportee can reject what should be properly accepted—or the reverse. The channel of transmission can malfunction.

However, in actual practice, we frequently have recourse to another line of consideration; namely, source reliability. In many cases we ourselves simply do not possess enough information or sufficient expertise to make an informed judgment on such matters and are largely or wholly dependent on the reliability of a reporting informant. In these circumstances our acceptance of a report will depend not on our evaluation of its substance but rather on our evaluation of its source. If the source is deemed reliable, we will accept what it claims; if it is deemed unreliable, then we won't accept what it claims.

The transmission of information via intermediate sources—especially intermediaries that might intermingle interpretation or even misinterpretation with mere reportage—is clearly a situation that presents potential problems, not only of distortion but even of mere misunderstanding. It is always preferable to have *Z*'s *ipsissima verba* than to have *X* reporting that *Y* told him what *Z* said. It is not the law alone that looks upon hearsay with disfavor. Proximity to sources is a significant asset of reports.

To be sure, particular problems will arise in this context if the report at issue emanates from a source we deem to be highly reliable but yet is substantively doubtful on the basis of the information we otherwise have on the topic. When source reliability conflicts with report improbability, one is invariably perplexed. When the reverse is the case, there is, of course, no problem: one simply ignores the report.

Sources are not sacrosanct. As standards of the law have long recognized, even eyewitness reports are often unreliable.[1] Reports, however promising, should always be seen as *offering* rather that *giving*. Looking into the horse's mouth is never inappropriate here.

One cannot obtain credible reports without credible sources: *ex nihilo nihil fit*. Reports present information obtained from sources that could be human (observers) or documentary (other reports) or even instrumental (sensors or devices like thermometers, barometers, Geiger counters, watches, etc.), and sources can be more or less accurate and more or less reliable. And even as one cannot squeeze blood from a turnip, one cannot extract reliable information from an unreliable source.

The stars and tea leaves do not speak to us directly. Their reportage requires human interpretative intermediaries. And this is true not only for such oracular sources but also for technical monitors as well. The significance of barometer comportment, burglar alarms, electric meters, scenography's, and even watches require human interpretation to convey their informative message. The point is that instruments don't report, humans report on the basis of the comportment of instruments.

While human observers constitute a major source of information, even eyewitness testimony is potentially flawed. For a reporter cannot state the facts as such, but he or she can convey only what he or she thinks them to be. Then too there looms the distinction between first-hand information and "mere hearsay." Overall, even our "well-informed sources" can go astray.

With expertise, as with much else, there is a distinction between appearance and reality, between being regarded as an expert and actually being one. And sometimes apparent sources are just that, mere cognitive illusions. They can be rogues acting on their own or even "plants" that have infiltrated the setting to foster erroneous conclusions. And sometimes mere self-delusion is at work. As with everything else we do, simple human error can afflict reporting as well.

There is one sort of report that seems to lack a definite source; namely, rumor. Here the reporting issues impersonally from the vox populi: "It is widely believed that . . ." or even "Many people are persuaded that . . ." The source is unidentifiable. It is Dame Rumor who speaks. What we actually know in such cases is less a matter of what the facts are than a matter of what the facts are believed to be. The label "handle with care" should be attached to such reports.

Rumor is a matter of haphazard transmission. And as the report moves along a chain of transmission, there is at each stage the prospect of modification—of distortion or exaggeration. The claims of reports based on rumor are virtually impersonal and atmospheric, with no visible means of inaugurating support. In evaluating them we have to rely on considerations of evidentiation and plausibility alone. And rumor readily leads to news inflation, setting in motion a chain of escalation somewhat along the lines of "sick $\Rightarrow$ severely ill $\Rightarrow$ at death's door $\Rightarrow$ deceased," until at last one reaches Mark Twain's "The reports of my death are gravely exaggerated."

When someone is the ultimate author of a report—rather than merely its meditative transmitter—then their report is problematic if he or she is not *knowledgeable* about the matter. One can put no reliance on a report whose message indicates that the reporter does not "know whereof he speaks" and can thereby not speak authoritatively and accurately on the matter. A credible report will ideally issue from an informed authority. And the best way for a reporter to ground their claims in this regard is through a track record of good performance.

On the other hand, it will sometimes be critical to conceal not only the original source of the reported information but also even the identity of the reporter transmitting it. Periodically, this foray of secrecy is characteristic of counterespionage operations.

It has long been recognized that journalists make good information agents and spies because, in the course of mastering their craft, they learn the art of cultivating sources. The importance of source reliability in matters of military and diplomatic intelligence is indicted by the use of descriptors such as: "From a usually reliable source" or "From a biased source." When there is no reason to suspect deception, intercepted enemy communications can be classed as "highly reliable." The more that is known about the source of a report's information, the better can the recipient appraise its reliability. Of course the best source of all is "the horse's own mouth." The interception of an opponent's own reportage has always provided invaluable intelligence. For here there is presumably "no need, as with agents, to wonder about the good faith of the source and the soundness of his judgement."[2]

Sources will of course have to have some way of getting at the information they report—observations, documentation, further sources, or *something*. But usually report recipients cannot penetrate through to the deeper grounds of their reporting but are limited to dealing with what their sources provide. And their only means of assessing the knowledgeability and reliability of their sources is principally a matter of the accuracy of the reporter's track record with regard to the relevant issues.

In many if not most military contexts good and reliable sources are hard to come by and must be carefully nurtured. This can create a conundrum in contexts of espionage, when using a source's information would compromise its identity—and thereby its future availability. Thus, in the Second World War the Allies went to great lengths during the Battle of the Atlantic to mislead the Germans into thinking that the effectiveness of their submarine locating was due to innovative electronic detection devices rather than having broken into the location-reporting communications used by the submarine command.

Conscientious reporters will generally be explicit about attribution, ascribing the informative claims of these reports to the sources from which they derive. Only in this way can the recipients of reports evaluate their credibility with high confidence. Often, however, these sources (for good reason) cannot or should not be specifically identified. In this event they should, however, be evaluated—as usually reliable, problematic, new and contrived, or whatever other characteristic may be useful and appropriate.

It is clear that the reportee who is in a position to bestow rewards or penalties on reporting is in a position to have greater confidence in the accuracy of reportage. Innumerable factors are at work in motivating people to provide information to others. Making reports can be part of one's job, motivated by payment, acts of gratitude, means to achieve fame and fortune, acts of public spirit; the list goes on and on.

The recipient of a report may or may not have knowledge regarding the report's sources. When he or she does so and has trust in the reporter, then they will give credence to the report in accordance with their evaluation of these sources. In general, reporters do well to attest to the reliability of their sources. For no reporter is ever in a position to guarantee the complete and unqualified acceptance of their reports. Acceptance is always something that lies in the province of the recipient. All that a reporter can ever do is put this reportage into the most persuasive and ingratiating form.

In many contexts the maintenance and nurturing of sources calls for protecting their confidentiality by keeping their identity hidden. This sort of thing is particularly critical in journalism, in espionage, in whistle-blowing, and in exploiting "insider information." In such situations there is bound to be a good deal of tension between confidentiality and protection, on the one hand, and, on the other hand, establishing the credibility of the information at issue—a factor for which knowing the identity of the source is critical. But even in cases where reporters do not identify their sources, they are well advised to provide the reportee with information tending to establish their credibility.

In matters of individual conflict reportage about one's enemy's plans and intentions is especially valuable. Providing this is greatly helped by being in touch with them. But this raises problems of trust. It is difficult to know what to make of unwilling competitors from the other side—defectors or mysterious visitors like Rudolf Hess. But the fact remains that, as Sir Stewart Menzies (designated C), the head of British intelligence during the Second World War, put it bluntly, "All sophisticated intelligence services maintain contact with their enemies."[3] And when it comes to making peace, their role can be invaluable.

Sources that provide useful information that is not otherwise available are of special value. Not only (by hypothesis) is the information itself helpful in such a case but also there is the collateral benefit of attesting to the reliability and future utility of this source.

A great deal depends on whether one's sources are independent or function under a common influence. When this happens, one should simply treat that group of reciprocally influenced sources as constituting a single unit.

With independent sources the situation is very different however. For these effectively function as a pathway to increased reliability. With dependent sources we are in a situation of "the chain is no stronger than its weakest link." With independent sources, by contrast, one is in the situation of a rope whose threads support and reinforce one another to create a result stronger than any constituent alone. And so the best-credentialed reports are those that emanate from a plurality of independent sources—even when those sources, taken individually, are not all that reliable. Consilience of reporting suggests a commonality of focus that cannot be dismissed as "mere coincidence."

In espionage there is always a distance between what one can practicably obtain via the assets in place and what one would ideally like to have. And there is a natural reluctance to redeploy an asset with assured access to reliable information on one topic into a position of dubious access to another potentially more desirable topic, trading a bird in hand for one in the bush. Certainly agents in the field are unlikely to enter into such redeployment save being under pressure from their control center back home.

REPORTER ISSUES

A clear understanding of the information needs and priorities of the reportee is a cardinal desideratum with reporters. Beyond this, two modes of merit are basic with respect to reporters their *knowledgeability* and their *trustworthiness.*

The standard use of reports is to convey information. But the way in which this objective is pursued opens the door to other aims as well. For reporters can have an agenda of their own. This circumstance opens the door to the sort of thought manipulation generally characterized as *propaganda*—the skewing and starting of reportage to cast a favorable (or, as the case may be, unfavorable) light upon people, countries, institutions, policies, and so on. With the facts qualified by terms of laudation or derogation, and the steady drumbeat of repeated harping on particular matters, the recipient of the correlative reportage becomes browbeaten into seeing matters in a prejudicial, and thereby erroneous, light.

One of the prime facets of reporter credibility relates to expertise. Especially when a report relates to technical, industrial, or scientific matters, it is constructive for the reporter to be knowledgeable in the area, able to monitor both relevancy and accuracy. Thus in the case of the Soviet Union's Manhattan Project espionage it proves vital that their main informant was Klaus Fuchs, one of the most senior scientists in the theoretical physics division at Los Alamos. Expertise is a matter of establishing authority; it pivots on presuming the correctness in regard to the judgments of those "experts" within the domain of their expertise who do not—should not—extend beyond a particular, well-defined range of subject matter. Any sensible recourse to experts must recognize that there are proper limits here because ample experience teaches that expertise does not carry over from one area to another.

A reporter is treated as an authority insofar as one accepts their reports on a given subject without further ado. However, two importation caveats must be made here. The first is that expertise is highly topical in nature: again, it does not carry over form one field to another. Moreover, acknowledged expertise is an artefact of perception and reception—of how widely that individual's claims to credibility are acknowledged among otherwise knowledgeable people. Reputation is the key to the acceptance of expertise. Established expertise does indeed provide the basis for a presumption—but an ultimately defeasible presumption—of correctness in the case at hand. But this presumption is defeasible and it's bearing tentative. In accepting it as valid in the particular case we take a step for which, in the final analysis, it is we ourselves—and neither the expert nor the generality that acknowledges him or her as such—who are ultimately responsible. The acceptance of expert advice is a very sensible step, but when all is said and done it is something that *we do on our own responsibility* and must therefore stand subject to the relevant sorts of safeguards. A person's reputation as an expert is no more than *evidence* of this individual's credibility regarding the matters at hand.

One must distinguish, moreover, between *originating* and *transmitting* reports, with the former originally providing the reprinted information and the latter merely passing it along. An author-attributed newspaper report merely transmits the information provided by its on the spot reporter, and thus its report is limited by that reporter's credibility. In espionage there is often an expedition or "agent-controller" who merely forwards the information provided by the agents. Knowledgeability about the information or topic at issue is significant with report initiation, but with report transmission it is dispensable.

Access to information is a critical requisite from a reporter's point of view. Without it there cannot be anything to report. And access often requires deceit—especially in matters of political or military intelligence. Here reporters who seek the "cover" of anonymity—especially spies—favor casting themselves as journalists to reach their many-sided curiosity from suspicion.

A reporter who does not report is clearly of no account. But what if there is nothing new to report? There is then little alternative but to resort to "filler." The newspaper correspondent can turn to "human interest" stories. The spy has a choice; he or she can pass along rumors and current gossip or simply make things up—with the latter apparently the preferred alternative.[4]

THE RELIABILITY OF REPORTING

As mentioned above, the acceptability of a report depends on the reliability of its sources, and we ourselves often do not have enough information or expertise to make an informed judgment, thus making us dependent on the reliability of a reporting informant. In these circumstances our acceptance of a report depends not on our evaluation of its substance but on our evaluation of its source: if a report's source is deemed reliable, we accept its claims; if unreliable, we do not accept its claims.

A key problem arises in this context if the report at issue emanates from a source we deem to be highly reliable but is substantially doubtful on the basis of the (presumably intensive) information we have on the topic. When source reliability conflicts with report improbability, one is going to be perplexed. And whether the reporter is providing information or disinformation, the reporter wants in any case to achieve the reliably needed for the acceptance of reports, be this a matter of fact or of illusion.

Even reports that transmit nothing but truths can be problematic: their message can be perfectly argued but nevertheless prejudiced, slanted, or judiciously contrived to mislead. This is especially relevant when the reporter has a stake in evoking a certain reaction on the reportee's part. Whenever such an interest exists, the reporter is well advised to declare it and take suitable countermeasure to having his reportage discounted. The Roman proverb "I should not believe such a story were it told me by Cato" holds true.

A reporting agent who, for any reason, plays fast and loose with the information of their report cannot be relied upon. This reporter becomes *discredited*. Like astrology with its reportage of messages written in the stars, unreliable reporters find it difficult to gain a hearing in the ears of sensible people. Bias throws trustworthiness into question. In light of this circumstance, we witness the frantic and elaborate disinformation campaigns launched by the Soviets to misrepresent the atomic weapon espionage of the Rosenberg group and the diplomatic-political espionage of Alger Hiss as nothing but trumped-up McCarthyite anticommunist hysteria.

Still, the recipient of a report must bear in mind that there is always a possible disconnection between what the reporter actually observes (say a strange light configuration in the sky) and what interpretation he or she places upon this in forming his or her report. Spies of course exploit this difference so as to make correct interpretation of their reportable actions difficult. (It is hard to tell an accidental encounter from a planned rendezvous.)

Then there is not only the problem of getting misleading information from reporters who impose their biases on what they report but also that of sources with an agenda of their own that distorts reported information. When sources lack good credentials, their reports will have little value! And then too there is the problem of corrupt sources, such as the agent who has been "turned" and is induced to provide misinformation.

It is critical that a report actually comes from the individual who purports to be its sender.[5] Much can go wrong with sources, and there is a great deal to worry about reports on this score. Britain's chief intelligence officer in France during the First World War "followed the simple and sound rule that no information should be accepted as probable unless it was confirmed by at least two independent sources."[6] It is a matter of balancing risks.

Even in cases where reporters do not identify their sources, they are well advised to provide the reportee with information tending to establish their credibility. A reporter must be ever mindful that from the recipient's point of view there is a potential gap between the real truth and what someone purports to be such. For credibility, a report must be reliable alike in substance and in provenience. If a recipient is to profit from a reporter's information, the recipient must have the trust to accept what it says at face value. And to this end, there is no better assurance than a track record of good performance on the reporter's part.

However, even if only 20 percent of a reporter's claims in some domain are true (so that any given assertion has a low a priori probability), and then if a certain contention follows from each one of the considerable multiplicity of its claims, then it is nevertheless promisingly probable. And similarly, if a multiplicity of individually problematic sources independently agree on reporting something, then this is quite likely to be true.

To be sure, we sometimes accept—no doubt cautiously, reluctantly—reports from sources that have no track record at all or one that is insufficient and indecisive. But this is something of an act of desperation. When we badly need a report's information and have no alternative way of obtaining it and no independent way of checking it, we may have no option but to clutch at this straw.

With report acceptance, responsibility simply cannot be offloaded. It follows the individual like their own shadow. The individual who gives credence to a report is always the responsible decider. It is he or she who acknowledges that authority, adopts its counsel, and accepts it on this occasion. The "just following advice" excuse is even less exculpatory of responsibility than is its cousin of "just following orders." Treating you as an authority whose reports are to be taken at face value is something that is done by me and not you. When X treats Y as authoritative, it is indeed Y who is responsible for the reports but X who is responsible for their acceptance.

The most reliable reports are all too often those one is not intended to see. In conflict situations, intercepting the confidential reports among well-informed opposition officials can generally provide information of high quality. Thus, the Allies best information about affairs in Germany during the Second World War came from covertly intercepting reports sent from Berlin to Tokyo by Lieutenant General Hiroshi Ōshima, Japan's ambassador to Germany and a trusted persona grata with various high-ranking Nazis, including the Führer himself.[7]

While reliability is an indispensable merit with reports, accuracy of detail is no less crucial a factor. A watch may be totally unreliable as to seconds and yet highly reliable as to hours. Such issues of detail are key to assessing the track record of a source's reliability. But even the accepted report of a knowledgeable source has little value if the circumstances are such that little confidence can be put upon these factors.

Regrettably, there is a good deal more to this crucial matter of a track record than meets the eye. For appraising a reporter's track record calls for scrutinizing their performance in comparable cases. And this issue of comparability is generally debatable. And even after a reference class of kindred cases has been settled in, the issue of perceptual circumstances can always arise. All in all, track record assessment is a matter less of automaticity than of judgment.

The sagacious reporter will accordingly take due care to safeguard their credibility. However, whenever one of a nation's espionage agents is unmasked, its intelligence agencies go to great lengths to convince the enemy to consider the spy as a "plant" intended to provide misinformation so as to undermine the agent's trustworthiness as a source, thereby negating the reliability of any secrets betrayed.

"You are well advised to accept what an otherwise reliable reporter claims to be so" is a sound principle of practical procedure. But it is not totally validated by the objective facts of the matter: It is not flatly true that presumptively "reliable" reports always speak truth. In general, however, we adopt an epistemic policy of credence in the first instance because it is the most promising avenue toward our goals, and then we persist in it because we subsequently find, not that it is unfailingly successful, that it is highly cost-effective.[8]

A characteristic difficulty arises when a potential recipient awaits a report that is simply not forthcoming. It is hard to interpret the absence of an expected report. Has something gone wrong with the reporter? Has the report been sent but somehow gone amiss in transit? Was there nothing to be reported? Silence is highly equivocal and difficult to interpret: in the circumstances the reporter does well to account for it. Some of the standard presumptions generally at work in matters of conscientious reporting are that the reporter

- reports the truth as he or she sees is
- reports the importantly relevant facts known or readily secured
- pays due heed to matters of timeliness (i.e., does not report today what would and should have been transmitted yesterday)

The communicative policy of adopting such presumptions, in the absence of any case-specific counterindications, is in place because it is always in our interest to proceed in ways that are efficient and effective in meeting our informational requirements. If playing safe were all that mattered, we would, of course, suspend judgment indefinitely. But it is simply not in our interest to do so, since safety is not everything. A policy that would deprive us of any and all communicative benefit is inherently counterproductive.

REPORTER ASSETS

Some reporter merits are pervasive—informativeness and conscientiousness among them. Others are context-variable. Credible reports generally require reliable reporters. Even though it lies in the nature of the enterprise that we cannot ask that our reporting spies should be *honest*; they should be *trustworthy* vis-à-vis ourselves.

But of course we will not take this to be so on faith. For even a source that is well informed and generally reliable can be corrupted by undue influence of some sort. Self-interest, bribery, intimidation, or force majeure can impel a source into providing misinformation. The reliability of reporters is largely a matter of their track record—but not entirely. For people can be deflected from their usual course by various sorts of motivating influences. Not only can a reporter grow careless over time but also corruption, manipulation, and undue influence can produce distortion. (In the case of espionage, for example, a reporting agent can be "turned.")

Among reporters of all sorts, it is perhaps spies that require the greatest array of skills. Ideally, a secret service will want its spies to be:

- *linguistically variable* (to enlarge the range of potential informants and cognitive access)
- *extensively knowledgeable* (to provide access to information needed for the proper interpretation of discovered facts)
- *socially adept* (to have the people skills needed to facilitate contact with potential informants)
- *conscientiously dedicated* (to provide information extensively and reliably)

And no less important is being well placed in relation to sources of information. An agent positioned to get access to needed information can be excused for many faults (boorishness, insobriety slackness) through providing occasional burst of critical information. Tradecraft can be learned but great spies are the product of nature and circumstance rather than teaching—they are not produced but evolve naturally.

Reports relating to inherently controversial issues—UFO encounters, for example, or sightings of the Loch Ness Monster—are through this very fact doubtful and invite scrutiny and skepticism. For here the reporter becomes a strongly interested party—if accepted, his or her report would doubtless secure fame and fortune. A special problem arises whenever a reporter has a strong personal interest in the acceptance of their reports. This obviously creates a suspicion of standing and distraction. At the very least such an interest should be both overtly declared and counteracted by extra pains to produce independent information.

The process through which a reporter's trustworthiness is built up in matters of information development and management is best understood by means of an economic analogy that trades on the dual meaning of the idea of credit. For we proceed in cognitive matters in much the same way that banks proceed in financial matters. We extend credit to others, doing so at first to only a relatively modest extent. But beyond this initial and presumptive benefit of doubt, trust has to be earned. When and if they comport themselves in a manner that shows that this credit was well deserved and warranted, we proceed to give them more credit and extend their credit limit, as it were. By responding to trust in a responsible way, one improves one's credit rating in cognitive contexts much as in financial contexts. The same sort of mechanism is at work in both cases: recognition of credit worthiness engenders a reputation on which further credit can be based; earned credit is like money in the bank, well worth the measures needed for its maintenance.

Thus, in the end, report communication is a commercial system of sorts. Credit is extended, drawn upon, and, when all goes well, enlarged. And with communicative and financial credit alike, one could not build up credit (prove oneself creditworthy) unless given *some* credit by somebody in the first place. For credit to be obtainable at all, there has to be an initial presumption that one is creditworthy. In communicative contexts too, such a presumption of innocent until proven guilty—free of fault until shown to be otherwise. To be sure, such a presumption can be defeated; one can of course prove oneself to be unworthy of credit or credence. But nevertheless, the operation of those presumptions "as a rule" is critical for the viability of the entire communicative enterprise.

Trust is, of course, something that we can have not only in people but also in cognitive sources at large. For a not dissimilar story holds for our information-generating technology—for telescopes, microscopes, computing machinery, and so on. We initially extend some credit because we simply must, since they are our only means for a close look at the moon, at microbes, and so on. But subsequently we increase their credit limit (after beginning with blind trust) because we eventually learn, with the wisdom of hindsight, that this is warranted. Over time the course of experience indicates, retrospectively as it were, that we were justified in deeming them creditworthy. And in this regard the trustworthiness of people and the reliability of instruments are closely analogous.[9] But overall the instrumental motivating of electronic processes (so-called SIGNIT, signals intelligence) is often more informative and reliable than the processing of human reports (so-called HUMINT, human intelligence).[10]

To be sure, the risk of deception and error is present throughout our cognitive endeavors, and our reports are cognitive instruments that, like all other instruments, are never fail-safe. In national security matters trust is essential and the historical record illustrates the problems here. The instances of Richard Sorge in Tokyo, of Anthony Blunt in London, or of Alger Hiss in Washington all illustrate that it is far from easy to spot a wolf in sheep's clothing. The practitioners of counterespionage have their work cut out for them. Still, a general policy of judicious trust is eminently cost-effective. In inquiring, we cannot investigate everything; we have to start somewhere and invest credence in something. But of course our trust need not be blind. Initially bestowed on a basis of mere hunch or inclination, it can eventually be tested and then come to be justified with the wisdom of hindsight. And this process of testing can in due course put the comforting reassurance of retrospective validation at our disposal.

REPORTING LIMITS

Does reporting have limits? For better or worse, the answer is clearly "yes." There indeed are limits and actually various different kinds thereof.

- *Limits of decency and decorum.* The *New York Times* motto "All the news that's fit to print" clearly indicates the existence of such limits.
- *Limits of trust.* One does not—should not—report on the confidences of people. The confidentiality of the confessional is absolute. Physician-patient interactions are sacrosanct.
- *Limits of confidentiality.* Personal financial information is restricted. Identity theft is theft.
- *Limits of prudence.* Reports do well not to give hostages to fortune. FDR's supporters were careful to avert reportage that portrayed him as a cripple.

With each limiting category there are the questions of range—of whether and how these limits might themselves have limits. But in each case it is clear that *there are limits*, even though occasionally unclear of just where they begin and end.

It is unfortunate but true that reporting can serve as a mode of cognitive warfare, with reports functioning as assault weapons for discrediting people or ideas. In this regard, leaking prejudicial reports is a favored recourse. Especially in matters of political and public affairs, the all too familiar process of "hate campaign" reporting has always played a prominent role.

CHAPTER 3
CONTENT MATTERS

KEY REPORT VIRTUES

The infinitely complex relationship between reality as it is and what it is thought to be constitutes one of the most challenging issues of informative reportage. To illustrate the nature of the problems that arise, it suffices to use the overly simple situation of a 3 × 3 grid with entries 0 and 1 as per the following illustration.

REALITY (THE ACTUAL SITUATION)			APPEARANCE (REALITY AS REPORTED)		
0	0	0	1	1	0
1	1	0	?	?	1
1	1	0	0	0	1

With "?" indicating a lack of information, errors of *omission*, there can of course also be errors of *commission*—and observe that in this example not one single piece of basic information (i.e., grid entry) is error-free. Nevertheless, even this "totally incorrect" picture of the situation somehow manages to convey a great deal of correct information, namely:

- Every row (and every column) contains both an 0 and a 1.
- One and only one diagonal uniformly has the same entry-value.
- At least one row has exactly two 1s.

Accordingly, even so simple an example indicates that even gravely deficient reports can (in theory) convey a great deal of correct information. (And the reverse is the case even with substantially correct reports.)

Clearly, the greater the discrepancy between appearance and reality, the bigger the problems that arise. And the more our questions-resolutions enter into the detail of things, the more error prone we become. Yet all the same, the correctness of our reportage across a wide and varied range clearly affords our best-practicable test of its overall value.

A prime aim of reporting is to provide information that is of use to the reportee. However, report content is determined by the reporter. As in tunnel building, the enterprise will succeed only if its two sectors manage to connect. This situation makes good reporting into a profoundly collaborative venture. And in consequence a considerable array of critical distinguishing factors serve to differentiate good and useful reports from poor and useless ones, with the following being preeminent: veracity; informativeness; accuracy; plausibility; adequacy; clarity, detail, and precision; evidentiation; impartiality and unvarnished factuality; reinforcement and redundancy; visibility and saliency; actionability; timeliness; and security. We'll now look at each factor in some depth.

Veracity

Veracity is a paramount desideratum of reports. Ideally, true propositions (and true propositions only) would be accepted, and false propositions (and false propositions only) would be rejected. But this is not an ideal world, and missteps can occur, in matters of reportage as elsewhere. The errors are principally of two sorts:

- *Errors of the first kind:* to reject what should be accepted (i.e., true propositions)
- *Errors of the second kind:* To accept what should be rejected (i.e., false propositions)

Seeing that there is no direct way to access the truth save via the process of inquiry, the occurrence of error (of both kinds!) is virtually inevitable. The two kinds of errors stand in a relationship of teeter-totter balance. In seeking to avoid the errors of one kind (be it the first or second), we will automatically increase errors of the other kind. All the same, the rational person strives for an optimally constructed belief manifold, one which overall balances errors of commission and omission to the greatest extent realizable in the circumstances at hand. But the regrettable reality of it is that we pay for the reduction of errors of one kind by the increase in errors of the other. In the circumstances in which we do and must work, perfection—the annihilation of error—is simply unrealizable; all we can do is to keep the total down to the lowest achievable level. Seeing that there is no unqualifiedly categorical assurance here, we just "have to take our chances."

In the end, the practice of taking the probable, plausible, or well substantiated as actually true is not more than a reasonable hope. But it is effectively unavoidable, although in accepting the probable, well evidentiated, and so on as true, one is implementing a reasonable policy of practical procedure.

INFORMATIVENESS

Its informativeness reflects the extent to which a report provides information on relevant issues relating to the topics at issue. This is, in a familiar way, a matter of the substantive breadth and depth of content. But there is also the related issue of novelty: of the extent to which they put our understanding of the relevant issues into a new light and a more instructive perspective. (A very informative report may nevertheless present only "old news.")

An adequate understanding of reportage must come to terms with human deviousness. For of course reports can be contrived not only to inform but to mislead: They can convey not just information but misinformation as well. And this can be done not only with a view to the report's intended recipient but also with a view to misleading the otherwise nonstandard recipients who intercept the report. This is, of course, a not infrequent and often effective practice with respect to military operations. The elaborate reportage mounted for Patton's nonexistent army group in early 1945 for an invasion operation across the Pas-de-Calais is a vivid example of the moral descriptive malreporting.

Accuracy

Accuracy in reporting is a matter of "getting it right." In assessing accuracy, some of the other prime desiderata for reports will come to the fore. The U.S. military in Hawaii received several war warnings from Washington during November 1941. By December some of the glitter began to fade,[1] and when nothing untoward happened, the accuracy of the reportage fell into doubt. Accuracy, like truth, is something one cannot tell from the substance of a report itself. A report cannot function as judge and jury in its own case. Its correctness will at best be assessed obliquely via various features that can be assessed through a complex venture in coordination and exploitation.

PLAUSIBILITY

The plausibility of a report in the prevailing context is critical for its credibility. A report that goes counter to established fact and common knowledge is thereby automatically unacceptable. Accordingly, for a report to be acceptable the reported information must be *plausible*—it must be believable in the context of the prior information accepted by the recipient: to be seen as acceptable, a report must not be too strongly counterindicated by background information. For reports are never context free and isolated. They invariably fall into contexts of preestablished acceptance—if not those provided by other reports, then by a more general framework of relevant background information. And here harmonization and systemic fit enter into the discussion. Accordingly, source reliability is not everything with reports: it is a necessary but not sufficient condition for acceptability. From a recipient's point of view, the credibility of a report is largely a function of its relation to its context. If this relationship is harmonious and the report accords smoothly with the otherwise available information, then its credibility is automatically enhanced. On the other hand disagreement, dissonance, and conflict are red flags that compromise credibility. Those interested in fostering the misinformation of false reportage will of course make use of this situation and take care to embed it in a wide setting of supportive "chatter."

All the same, dismissing counter-expectation reports on grounds of diminished credibility should never be the end of the matter. The issue of dismissal should be seen as a problem that calls for resolution. Where that matter at issue is important, some effort should be made to explain—or explain away—that discord. For there is sometimes good reason why it is not the dismissed report but the earlier impression that is at fault.

Sometimes the medium itself conveys the message. If you are expecting a telephone call from X (and no one else), then the mere ringing of the phone—the activation of the connecting linkage—itself conveys the reporting message: "X is on the line, calling." And the same holds with various automatic reporting devices, such as fire alarms.

ADEQUACY

The information of a report shall ideally not just be incurred but also meet a certain level of *adequacy* with regard to the relevant issues: reports should ideally meet the same standards as court testimony in providing "the truth, the whole truth, and nothing but the truth." In large part actual reports at least purport to satisfy this aspiration regarding what the reportee sees as highly relevant—laying claim to a completeness that is, to be sure, not absolute but sufficient to meet the needs of the situation at hand.

If I call 911 to inform the police that someone is climbing into my neighbor's house, the report would be gravely flawed if I omitted mentioning that I saw this person to be armed.

CLARITY, DETAIL, AND PRECISION

Clarity is another prime value of reports. A report that is vague, imprecise, or equivocal is close to useless.

The oracle at Delphi was notorious for issuing equivocal reports. According to Herodotus, Croesus, the king of Lydia, consulted the Delphine oracle regarding a projected attack on the Persian Empire. Told that "If you cross the river, a great empire will fall," Croesus mistakenly gave a favorable interpretation to this "oracular" pronouncement. A report that speaks its message with forked tongue might as well keep silent. A useful report must offer its message with sufficient detail to be grasped, checked, and implemented.

When Japanese agents reported fleet movements at Pearl Harbor, they helpfully provided not only the presence of ships in the port but also details about berthing locations. This provided a clear sign that "they knew what they were talking about."

The extent of detail is obviously a significant feature of reports. Thus, consider the report of a troop movement stating that it involved

- a large body or
- four divisions or
- three infantry and one mechanized division

The final more detailed report clearly has some important virtues. Not only does it convey more information but also the very fact of its doing so enhances its credibility by indicating that its source is both more authoritative (better informed) and more trustworthy (willing to put his claims to the test).

In matters of informative discourse, there is a crucial connectivity between precision and informativeness. If I want to know how many trees there are in the forest, it will not help to be told that there are "more than two"—however true this contention may be. If I want to know when the Great Pyramid of Giza was constructed, it will not help much to be told that it was before the battle of Waterloo—correct though that is. In matters of information we want not only truth and reliability but also detail and accuracy. There is a complementary trade-off between precision and informativeness on the one hand and tenability and probability on the other: when there is more of the one, there is proportionately less of the other. For this reason it is surprising that, while cognitive theorists have had a great deal to say about truth, the matter of precision—of detail and accuracy—is seldom if ever maintained by them.

It is a basic principle of epistemology that increased confidence in the correctness of our estimates can always be secured at the price of decreased accuracy. For in general an inverse relationship exists between the definiteness or precision of our information and its substantiation: detail and security stand in a competing relationship. We estimate the height of the tree at around 25 feet. We are quite sure that the tree is 25×5 feet high. We are virtually certain that its height is 25×10 feet. But we can be completely and absolutely sure that its height is between 1 inch and 100 yards. Of this we are "completely sure" in the sense that we are "absolutely certain," "certain beyond the shadow of a doubt," "as certain as we can be of anything in the world," "so sure that we would be willing to stake our life on it," and the like. For any sort of estimate whatsoever, there is always a characteristic trade-off relationship between the evidential security of the estimate (as determinable on the basis of its probability or degree of acceptability) and its contentual detail (definiteness, exactness, precision, etc.).

A crucial factor here is the preservation of truthworthiness and reliability. The operative principle is that of caution: supply no superfluous detail; do not aim at more accuracy and possession than the circumstance at hand requires. And the fact of it is that in practical matters we can often dispense with precision. To decide to carry an umbrella, one does not need to know just how many inches of rain there will be. To decide to invest in a stoc,k one need not sharpen your expectation of its rise to five decimal places. Medicaments are always prescribed in exact dosages, though there is generally no need for such precision here. In managing intelligence information it is wise to heed the words of Aristotle:

Our discussion will be adequate if it has as much clearness as the subject matter admits of, for precision is not to be sought for alike in all discussions, any more than in all the products of the crafts. Now fine and just actions, which political science investigates, admit of much variety and fluctuation of opinion, so that they may be thought to exist only by convention, and not by nature. . . . We must be content, then, in speaking of such subjects and with such premises to indicate the truth roughly and in outline, and in speaking about things which are only for the most past true and with premises of the same kind to reach conclusions that are no better. In the same spirit, therefore, should each type of statement be received; for it is the mark of an educated man to look for precision in each class of things just so far as the nature of the subject admits; it is evidently equally foolish to accept probable reasoning from a mathematician and to demand from a rhetorician scientific proofs.[2]

EVIDENTIATION

Evidentiation is clearly another critical factor with reports. The credibility of a report that contains data that helps to substantiate its information and support its claims is enhanced for this very reason.

When Richard Sorge, the Soviet master spy in Tokyo, reported to Moscow in 1941 that Japan had then no indication of attacking Asiatic Russia, he was able to cite concrete steps being taken to weaken Japanese forces in Manchuria. A skeptical Stalin, who had earlier dismissed Sorge's warning of the German invasion, now believed him and transferred some of the Soviet Union's Siberian division for the defense of Moscow.

Impartiality in presentation is a decidedly positive feature of reports. Being matter-of-fact without tendentious editorializing is of the essence here. A report whose presentation of the issues is tendentious and biased thereby undermines its credibility by raising questions, seeing that even without actual incorrectness it can nevertheless be misleading. Thus, during the Second World War, when the U.S. State Department's representatives in China reported the Nationalists' feeble hold on power, the higher authorities in Washington saw this as proceeding under the undue influence of the Chinese Communists' elaborate propaganda against Chiang Kai-shek's "Nationalist" regime. The partisan tenor of the reportage undermined its credibility.

And falsification, distortion, and slanting are not the only ways in which information transfer can be corrupted: suppression can also change the tenor of reportage. In Nazi Germany and in Soviet Russia the chiefs of the military intelligence services became increasingly reluctant to pass on to the man at the top information they thought would be unwelcome and troubling to him.

It is not for nothing that newspapers separate news from editorial commentary. News reporters are expected—and very rightly expected—to present "just the facts." And it comes to be recognized that editorial commentary of those facts is someone else's job—and often by someone not under the influence of the paper's ownership. No doubt the world's developments are to be considered as good, bad, or indifferent from various points of view. But however right- or wrong-minded such evaluation may be, it is not the reporter's job to provide it. Reportage should ideally be non-tendentious and value-free. Even when secret intelligence reporting is concerned, this view of the matter is generally taken by professionals—except in cases where it is altogether anathema to the person at the top when this happens to be a Hitler or a Stalin.

Reinforcement and Redundancy

There is also the important factor of statistical reinforcement. When many reports arrive from independent sources, this can and should be treated as a single circumstantially plausible report issuing from a reliable source. A report whose information overlaps with others provided by independent sources thereby substantially acquires greater credibility. A great deal of individually useless "chatter" can thus metamorphose into a decidedly reliable report. But while such reconfirmation is always welcome, its opposite—disagreement, conflict, and "mixed messages"—are always obstacles to the acceptability of a report.

Visibility and Saliency

A report can only do its proper work when it is recognizable amid the welter of events. Information inflow can be too much of a good thing. Overload can be a significant problem with reportage. It can become easy to lose sight of the significant needles in a large haystack. To be really useful, significant reportage should stand out above the environing plethora of trivial fact. In late 1941 there were innumerable reports of Japanese military activity throughout the western Pacific region, and it was clear that a naval blow was about to be struck. But the few signs that it might fall in Hawaii were easy to overlook amid the mass of signals.[3] In the end, precision of accuracy is a great virtue of reports. What might be called the Nostradamus effect lies in the trade-off between the detail of a report and its tenability, and it is tempting for reporters to seek security and safety in imprecision and vagueness.

ACTIONABILITY

Actionability is a matter of the extent to which reports can serve to shape and guide our course of action in relevant regards.

And the most useful reports are those that provide action-guiding information. The realization of such reports is the very reason for being of military and diplomatic intelligence. And it cuts both ways: early in the Second World War German interception of the position reports of Allied transatlantic convoys enabled Admiral Karl Dönitz's submarines to inflict punishing damage to them, but later intercepting the position reports of his submarines enabled the Allies to decimate his wolfpacks.[4]

TIMELINESS

Timeliness is a critical factor in the utilization of reports. The report of Andrew Jackson's victory at New Orleans reached the peace negotiators in Geneva well after the treaty ending the War of 1812 had already been signed, too late to affect the terms achieved by the United States. To all intents and purposes, old news is no news. When President Truman told Stalin about the atomic bomb at the Teheran summit, the Americans were surprised at the disinterest that Stalin exhibited. Little did they realize that the efficiency of his espionage services meant that Stalin's information about developments at Los Alamos was far more extensive and detailed than Truman's.[5]

SECURITY

The security of reporting is essential whenever it is important that reports reach their intended recipients and these recipients only. Thus, at the onset of the Second World War, Britain managed to round up and "turn" most of the German espionage agents in the United Kingdom. To preserve credibility, it had them also send amid disinformation a good deal of correct information arriving just too late for effective use.[6] We shall return to these issues of confidentiality in chapter 5.

REPORTAGE FEEDBACK AND DIALECTIC

The content of reports is usually determined by the reporter. In some cases, however—personal income tax reporting, for example, or the reports of financial institutions to regulatory agencies—the sort of information provided is mandated by the reportee. Sometimes effective reportage even calls for a dialectical back and forth between reporter and reportee that requires feedback regarding matters of amplification or further detail. The supplemental information provided through an interactive dialectic becomes especially useful when a need arises for reconciling conflicting reports. However, such chatter along the lines of transmission is undesirable whenever security is of the essence, seeing that it increases the choices of compromising not only the source but also the chain of transmission. Ideally reports should be self-sufficient, but here as elsewhere ideals are not invariably achievable.

REPORT PATHOLOGY

Misleading an opponent via incorrect information is one of the oldest tricks in the book. In warfare in particular deception is standard operating practice. Civil War generals put wooden canons on display; prior to the Normandy invasion in the Second World War, the Allies synthesized radio traffic for an entire nonexistent army group. Whenever information can go awry, so can reports. This brings three sorts of reporting malfunctions into view:

- *misinformation* that provides flatly false information
- *disinformation* that provides standard and misleading information
- *hyperinformation* that creates a destabilizing overload by virtue of its sheer mass

The reporting on a matter can be very misleading without containing any falsehoods. False impressions can be created not only by commission but also by omission. Reports on various matters can err—be it deliberately or by design—through leaving out essential points of detail. Completeness with respect to the relevant essentials is a pivotal merit.

Reports on Japan's movement of forces prior to the attack on Pearl Harbor was comprehensive and indicated movement to the south in the direction of the East Indies and the Kra isthmus. But there was little or nothing pointing eastward in the direction of Guam, Wake Island, Midway Atoll, or Hawaii—there is no indication as to where the initial blows were actually to fall.[7]

Whatever humans do can be done badly. And this holds as much for reporting as for anything else.

ON LYING AND DECEIT

David Hume maintained that we cannot accept the testimony of an interested witness, and Laplace reinforced this view with mathematical argumentation.[8] He concluded that if the witness has a personal stake in the issue, he or she will be tempted to lie, and that this circumstance will greatly reduce the probability that his or her contention is correct.

However, Laplace's reasoning is not without its problems. Consider the following two premises:

(1) X claims to have good evidence for maintaining p (e.g., that X saw p with his or her own eyes), and

(2) X lies; X actually has no good evidence on the issue but spoke from interest alone

From these premises, nothing whatsoever follows regarding the probability of p. The fact of it is that there are two sorts of "liars." One sort consists of those whose assertions are irresponsibly groundless and who thus manage to tell the truth with only random success. The other sort are those who deceitfully assert what they actually have good reason to deem false. Impropriety and "falsification" are involved in both cases. But in the first case what is misleading relates to the basis of one's claims, and in the second case what is misleading relates to the substance of one's claims. Both sorts of liars are untrustworthy but in rather different ways. A basis liar is truth-indifferent; a substance liar is truth-aversive. The latter avoids truth while the former ignores it. Lying of the one kind is a matter of blindness to the truth, lying of the other kind is a matter of falsity tropism—of outright deception.

Against this background, it transpires that the Hume-Laplace analysis turns on the stance that an interested witness proceeds with actual deceitfulness (i.e., "really knows better"). This seems farfetched. It requires that the witness knows the true facts and counterindicates them rather than merely being caught up in a self-deception that jumps to an ungrounded conclusion because "the wish is father of the thought." And this, of course, makes for a highly problematic substantive assumption.

CONFLICTING REPORTS

Conflicts are pervasive throughout the domain of reportage. The sponsors of a rally may report the presence of many thousands while their opponents put the count at a few hundred. At one point in the Second World War Admiral Dönitz's spies reported the ship *Queen Mary* in the Mediterranean while his radio monitors placed her in the South Atlantic.[9] In court trials each opposing side develops (very different) story lines by means of conflicting testimony regarding "who did what." In most situations where large amounts of information are processed, conflicting reports will make an appearance.

Sometimes such conflicts can be ameliorated by blending. When operative A reports a sighting as a movement of tanks while operative B reports it as a movement of personal carriers, the crucial fact may simply be the commonality of enemy forces being en route. Often, however, the clash is more drastic, as when A reports that X was present at the scene and B reports that X was not. We then have little choice but to follow the lead of the more reliable source or—in the case of effectively equal reliability—to favor the contextually more plausible report. Juries, police officers, intelligence analysts, historians, and innumerable other information processors are constantly required to do the best they can with conflicting reports.

Sometimes, to be sure, conflicts of reportage can be "explained away." If troops are being shipped from locations A to C via B, then a reliable reporter X, who is located on the arrival side of B, may reasonably report that B is being reinforced, while a reliable reporter Y who is located at the departure side of B, may report that B is being abandoned. In this sort of way, misinterpretation can engender conflicting reports. All too often the larger context, which provides "the big picture," is needed for the proper interpretation of reports. This is of particular importance in matters of national security intelligence, where the tendency to compartmentalize on a "need to know basis" is a counterweighting necessity.

In other ways, too, the issue of report content is not altogether as straightforward as it looks. Reports can often be viewed in a dual light as dealing with entirely separate issues. A physics textbook (say of 1890 vintage) can be seen as not only constituting a report on the natural processes of the universe but also as a report on the state of art prevailing in physics at that time. The nature of a report varies with the variation of what can be done about it.

With multiple reports there arises the vexing but all too common situation of mixed messages through the clash of conflicting reports. An issue must be decided one way or the other but the relevant reports range over a spectrum from strongly pro to strongly con. In dealing with such conflicting reports, one must obviously take account of the quantity and quality of the reports as per:

- the sheer number of independent reports inclining one way or the other
- the credibility of these reports in terms of the reliability of their sources
- the cogency of the evidentiation that these reports afford

A highly perplexing difficulty arises when there is not only a conflict in the message of the reports at hand but also a further clash as regards the factors of quality and quantity. This arises when the great majority of independent reports point in one direction while those of the highest individual quality point the other way.

The sensible resolution of report conflicts requires detailed knowledge of the relevant circumstances as well as good judgment. Conflict resolution is perhaps the most difficult and challenging comportment in the management of reports. The whole enterprise is fraught with risk. For even as victory does not always belong to the stronger battalions, so truth does not always belong to the strongest reportage. But when a decision has to be made one way or the other, this sort of thing seems to be the best one can do.

CHAPTER 4
TRANSMISSION

TRANSMITTING REPORTS

Reports are transmitted via an often complex process of conveying messages through a series of intermediaries. Even God resorted to symbolic intermediation via words resonating from clouds or bushes, angelic visitations, or inspiring dreams. Information does not move about of itself; its transfer from reporter to reportee must be provided by a mediating process of some sort. And only if this intermediation functions in an undistorted and uncorrupted way can information transfer be effective. (A regular system of information transmission by couriers and messengers was already in operation in imperial Rome.[1])

And not only must that communication reach its intended recipients, but when the information it conveys is ill formulated, the report as such does not arrive at all. A misunderstood "report" is no report at all. Appropriately accessible formulation is crucial.

Language is a complex and delicate instrument, which, as Charles Maurice de Tayllerand sarcastically put it, often seems to have been devised for the concealment of thought. In this light the faithful transmission of a report should itself never say more—but also never less—than what the report itself affirms.

The main vulnerabilities of modes of transmission are:

- *retardation* in failing to convey the report in a timely manner
- *distortion or corruption* in "garbling" the message being sent

- *insecurity* in being vulnerable to interception by unintended nonrecipients

Reports need not always be transmitted verbally. Often they can be conveyed by means of symbolic conventions, using such signals as "One if by land, two if by sea." However, the information being conveyed can always be formulated verbally and passed on in that format—ideally in a perspicuous way.

Reports must be accessible. They do us little good if we cannot send them. When he was Britain's foreign secretary in the nineteenth century, Lord Palmerston constantly urged his ambassadors to use darker ink to facilitate the legibility of their reports. The most informative of reports is useless if it does not reach its destination intact. The best and most successful spies working abroad cannot render useful service without the means for effective and secure transmission of their findings back to home base. And there is often the prospect of human or mechanical malfunction in the instrumentalities of transmission. Transmission processes that are erratic and unreliable—whose efficiency depends on the changeable whims of people, conditions of weather, fortunes of war, or the like—are to be avoided whenever possible.

Three factors are of prime importance with transmission: *reliability*, *timeliness*, and in many cases *confidentiality*.

Reliability of transmission is a major problem. Among other things, there are situations in which reporting relativity suffers through deliberate interference. Radio transmission can be jammed, postal or electronic communication disrupted, verbal communication prevented. The process of report transmission is not invariably easy and smooth.

Timeliness is a matter of minimizing the time lag between the source's emission and the recipient's access to the information it conveys. Some reports are given periodically at a particular time, like the traditional "noon whistle" at an industrial factory. Others are occasional. And some are temporally continuous and ongoing, like the location report of an auto's GPS system. But the most accurate and informative of reports will be useless if it arrives too late. In this regard there occurred a notable mishap in Japan's intended notification of the initiation of hostilities on December 7, 1941. The code room at the Japanese embassy in Washington was undermanned that Sunday morning so that the delivery of the report, scheduled for noon Washington time or 8 a.m. Hawaiian time, was not delivered to America's secretary of state until after 1 p.m., well over an hour after the start of the actual attack.[2]

Report confidentiality is the battleground for an ongoing arms race between those to whom report receipt is important and those for whom report penetration is advantageous. Transmission confidentiality can be protected in two major ways. One is by endeavoring to make the message itself inaccessible to outsiders (for example, via personal messengers, carrier pigeons). The other is by endeavoring to make the message unintelligible to outsiders (for example, via the use of codes and ciphers). Yet when the captain of a wolfpack submarine telegraphs a report of contact with a convoy, his message, though essential, renders his ship vulnerable to detection and attack. The decision to report often involves a choice between negatives.

For obvious reasons, it is a key principle of espionage reportage that reports not be traceable to reportees: that some sort of circuit breaker—a "dead drop" or obscurely invisible intermediary—be inserted into the transmission process between the reporting spy and the recipient at control center. The aim throughout is to conceal that the information is being transmitted, how it was obtained, and who supplied it. Report confidentiality is vulnerable at every stage. The reporter may be careless—or possibly even "turned." And the same holds for the recipient. But it is in the phase of transmission that report security is at its most vulnerable. One never knows who is listening in, and it is easy to underestimate their cleverness in figuring out the meaning of what they hear. Throughout the Second World War all of the German services had a fatally flawed confidence in the security of their Enigma coding machine,[3] alike in diplomatic, military, and naval communications. The process of transmission is generally the weakest link in the chain of espionage reportage. The very act can cause problems. And in transmitting uncertain information, a balance must be struck between evidential assurance and potential utility. Even a small probability that very useful information is correct may warrant its transmission. A reporter is well advised to play it safe and send potentially important information along with suitable caveats. Here acceptance and implementation rests with the recipient subject to the classic principle that caveat emptor.

It is of great advantage when one and the same individual is both the source of useful information and it's a reliable transmitter. Extraordinary in this regard is the case of Melita S. Norwood, who, as secretary to a senior official in Britain's atomic energy project ("Tube Alloys"), for years spent long nighttime hours laboriously encoding information on one-time pads and transmitting it to Soviet authorities from her modest semidetached house in South London's suburb of Bexleyheath. Here there was no need for complicated contact via dead drops and consular intermediaries—one dedicated and inconspicuous agent pretty much sufficed.

A crucial issue with respect to report transmission centers on the questions of the recipient's "right to know." Given the nature of the enterprise, a violation of this right is bound to have serious repercussions. (The matter of a "need to know" is something else again and involves other ranges of concern.)

If we are to communicate with others and keep them au fait with our thinking and ideas, we have to employ effective lines of communication. And this is virtually impossible when everything around us is collapsing, a situation that makes war-ending a process of vast difficulty. The yielding of army units is comparatively easy and facilitated by the traditional mechanism of flags of truce. But the yielding of nations requires a unity of command that is sometimes not readily available. (America's Civil War is a clear illustration: the several Southern armies negotiated their own surrender; the Southern nation never surrendered as such but simply faded away.)

Report transmission also has ethical aspects in view of the issues posed by the *New York Times* motto of "All the news that's fit to print." But these ethical issues lie outside the range of present concerns.

FLAWED TRANSMISSION

Reports transmitted in unusual ways—by newspaper notice, say, or by secret ink intermediation in ordinary letters—are of a nature where the medium is itself part of the message: "This is unusual stuff: pay special attention to it." This is notably the case with reports encrypted in high-security systems—a circumstance annoying to unintended recipients.[4]

Report transmission was easier in earlier times when reports were conveyed on paper rather than sent electronically; carriers were bribed, drugged, or deceived so that the messages they carried could be altered. For useful reportage, faithful transmission is essential. A report that is garbled, subject to static or interruption, cannot convey its message successfully: such a report is effectively no report at all. And in matters where security is a paramount concern, it is generally better not to send a report at all than to transmit it by unreliable means. Entrusting the transmission of a message to an unreliable messenger—be it personal or artefactual—is, accordingly, always ill advised. It demolishes all warrant for confidence that the message will convey its interested meaning and that it will reach its intended target—and those targets only.

Issues of security, secrecy, and confidentiality are crucial on report management. When X transmits reports to Y via channel C, the prospect that some third party Z has somehow modified or augmented or otherwise tampered with X's reports is generally an at least theoretical possibility. (In 1939 the German navy used its penetration of the French navy's communication system to issue falsified fleet orders in Admiral Darlan's name.[5])

In sending reports the availability of reliable lines of transmission is essential, and it is often useful to keep those resources available even between warring enemies. (Flags of truce were not invented for nothing.) And this is especially important when affairs are going badly and surrender is in prospect.[6]

Report transmission can be damaged by two major interventions: *culling* and *tampering*. With culling, the transmitter passes along only certain items in a way that compromises the overall reportage. This can be done deliberately, thanks to inadvertent misinterpretation on the mediator's point. Thus, on the morning of December 7, 1941, the soldiers monitoring a Hawaiian radar station chose not to report the sighting of a large incoming flight of aircraft because they mistook this for an expected flight of B-29 bombers from the United States instead of an attacking Japanese air armada.[7] With tampering, the message of the report is altered. Thus, at the end of the Pacific War when Japan's Foreign Office was desperately trying to indicate acceptance of the Potsdam declaration's unconditional surrender terms, it was fearful that the military channels of transmission on which its communications depended would sabotage the process by altering its messages.[8]

Targeted sending to interested recipients and unrestricted emission are importantly different commemorative situations. With targeted sending, there is also the presumption that certain individuals are *not* to have access to the report. And this can create difficulties.

For communications, vulnerability makes all the difference. In North Africa, German language communication had to go over the wireless and the Allies were able to take advantage. After the Normandy invasion, German communications could be managed by land lines and security became easier. To the chagrin of the Allies, the Ardennes offensive that issued in the Battle of the Bulge commenced wholly out of their hearing and the surprise achieved on this basis came as a costly shock.

Potentates and commanders often transmit reports via senior and trusted high-status intermediaries (ministers or ambassadors). Not only does this give added weight to the credibly of the reportage but also such intermediaries can be expected to know what is on their mind and thus be able to fill in what remains unsaid "between the lines" of the overt report. In these cases of special emissaries, there is an intricate symbioses between the messenger and the message. (Japan's decision to surrender was conveyed to major commands not just electronically from Tokyo but also by senior figures appearing in person—in some instances even members of the imperial family.[9])

However, information can be generally broken apart into subordinate components as when X will launch an attack tomorrow and Y will be its target. And this has important implications whenever security and confidentiality is of the essence. For then a breach in the wall of secrecy will mean that only a part of a report's information will be compromised rather than the whole of it. The spy who compartmentalizes his reports, forwarding the part derived from one source by a certain method and another part obtained elsewhere differently, will perhaps increase the chances of *some* interception but yet decrease the chances of a *total* compromise.

GENERAL (OPEN-ENDED) REPORT EMISSION

Unrestricted reporting emission that admits of universal access can result in a cognitive diffusion of information substantially akin to the epistemological spread of pathogens across a population. And many instructive analogies obtain here. For example, even as with an infection there are two related diffusion issues, exposure and succumbing, so with information there is receipt and acceptance (or endorsement), with the difference between the two determined by immunity in the one case and resistivity in the other.

For any of innumerable reasons, a report may fail to arrive, but even one that does so may fail to be believed. Accordingly, two very different types of report diffusion can be at work, *awareness* diffusion and *acceptance* diffusion. It is, after all, one thing to receive and access a certain report and something decidedly different to accept and endorse what that report declares. Different modes of unrestricted transmission have their own characteristic features. For example, rumors that spread person to person are notoriously prone to exaggeration.

Historically, when the open-ended reporting of major, cataclysmic developments is at issue, the process of information diffusion generally has the following structure:

- At first there is a very small group of initial reports of an almost hysterical character. (These invite skepticism partly by their very nature and tone and partly because of the universal and unexpected character of what is reported.)
- Subsequently, there arrives a modest number of amplifying reports that confirms what has been reported and provides some additional descriptive and explanatory detail.
- Finally, there comes an avalanche of further expository ma-

terial that eliminates any prospect of uncertainty or skepticism and constrains acknowledgment of what has heretofore seemed virtually unmanageable.

Washington's notification of the Pearl Harbor attacks, Stalin's notification of Germany's Operation Barbarossa, and Tokyo's notification of the atomic bombing of Hiroshima all exhibit this exact pattern of a powerful transition from incredulity to acknowledgment. To be sure, this situation has been altered by the speed and volume of reportage that present-day television news coverage makes possible—thus, with the 9/11 destruction of the Twin Towers, television coverage was so swift and graphic that people were virtually enabled to be eye-witnesses to the event—and this more traditional news media reportage is now being eclipsed by reports that are conveyed via social media outlets such as Twitter.

ISSUES OF TIMING AND URGENCY

Reports regarding the action and activities of parties of interest can differ in their temporal orientation. Specifically, they can relate to

- current activities,
- ongoing proceedings,
- long-range policies, and
- future plans

This difference in respect to timing has obvious implications for report processing, with those reports addressing issues of the nearer term deserving higher priority because time is a crucial factor when reaction is called for.

The time horizon of different modes of intelligence will clearly differ in point of urgency. With diplomatic intelligence and even more with economic espionage the matter of timing will usually not be all that crucial. But with military operations time is clearly of the essence and here intelligence generally focuses on the immediate future.

In many circumstances a report that arrives too late and conveys old news—whose information has been "overtaken by events"—is simply useless.[10] General Bernard Montgomery's chief intelligence officer observed that, "Military intelligence is always out of date, there is a built in time-lag. And better the best half-truth on time than the whole truth too late."[11]

Two different sorts of urgency are at issue with reports:

- *Consideration urgency*: urgency of processing, examination, and analysis—the urgency of addressing a report and gaining the information it provides.
- *Exploitation urgency*: urgency of implementation—the urgency of reacting to the report and actively doing something about it.

They are not identical but are obviously connected because exploitation presupposes consideration.

It might seem on first thought sensible to suppose that the recipient is the logical party to evaluate the consideration urgency of a report. But this supposition must be resisted. For by the time the recipient is in a position to carry out this evaluation, much water has generally passed under the bridge. When a report is really urgent, the sender is well advised to say so—albeit without creating a crying wolf situation by overuse.

Accordingly, with some reporting situations, it is crucial to determine who knows what—and when. One cannot hold someone responsible (be it legally or personally) for failing to act on a report they never received—or received only after the time for acting had passed. With many sorts of reports timeliness is of the essence. When a bomb threat is reported, one certainly wants to learn of it right away. And in financial matters, for example, it can be extremely advantageous to learn of new developments that can significantly impact the markets even a matter of seconds ahead of the competition.

In regard to timing, many reporting situations are geared to a repetitive periodicity, with regular reportage transpiring on a weekly, monthly, or yearly basis. Some are even continually ongoing in real time—the monitoring of temperature, for example, or the transaction prices on the New York Stock Exchange. With national security issues, this matter of report timing can be significant. Not long before the Pearl Harbor attack, Japan's port watchers there were instructed to accelerate their report on warship movements and anchorages from a weekly to a daily basis.[12]

In recent times reporting has enjoyed great advances in the efficiency of transmission owing to the increase in numbers and size of information providing organization and the increased speed of message transmission facilitated by modern communication technology.

TRANSLATION PROBLEMS

Translation is often an integral part of the transmission of reports. Nevertheless, reporting encounters potential problems whenever the message that arrives needs to be translated for the benefit of its recipients. For with translation, there is the prospect of many steps between cup and lip.

In dealing with reports, sagacious interpretation is sometimes able to atone for flawed translation. During the Battle of the Bulge, when the surrounded forces of General Anthony McAuliffe at Bastogne were summoned to surrender his response was "Nuts!" Duly reported, this caused some bafflement among the German translators, but the ultimate recipients had no difficulty figuring it out.

Whenever reports need to be translated, the substance of the report—literal meaning of its message—should ideally be preserved intact and unaffected. But translation generally poses characteristic difficulties because a very thin and permeable barrier separates translation from interpretation.

Translation from one language into another is in effect a process of information transmission. And things can readily go wrong here. As the Italian proverb puts it "*traduttore, traditore,*" to translate is to betray. It is clear that if a report needs to be recast in another language, great care must be taken in the first instance neither to add to nor to subtract from the information it conveys. Whatever supplementary interpreting or explanation the translator purposes to add should be clearly indicated and set part from the report itself. It may be useful to have such supplementation. But its provision not by the reporter but by the translator should be made explicit if optimal benefit from the report is to be attained.

Translation is particularly difficult where technical language that departs from ordinary usage is at work. In the Second World War England's codebreaking center at Bletchley Park developed ample facilities for putting intercepted German communication into English. But the Royal Navy insisted on getting all its material forwarded in the original German, firm in the conviction that only naval people would adequately grasp naval lingo.

Translation is often tantamount to interpretation. When Japan was groping its way toward surrender at the end of the Second World War, it became important to decide whether the Cairo Declaration of

1943 in requiring "the unconditional surrender of Japan" referred to the Japanese state as such or specifically to its military. The Potsdam Declaration of 1945 apparently clarified this in its explicit reference to "the unconditional surrender of all Japanese armed forces." This reconstrual played an important role in Japan's final deliberations, because the state was not presumed to surrender unconditionally since the abolition of Japan's imperial system was deemed unacceptable by everyone concerned in that country's deliberations.[13] Interpretation and translation became crucial issues with thousands of lives hanging in the balance.

TRANSMISSION SECURITY

Confidentiality in matters of state lies somewhere between difficult and impossible to achieve. The only way to gain assurance of the security of one's system is by endeavoring to penetrate it. But doing this with the same determination and resource commitment that the enemy is prepared to dedicate to the project is a virtually unattainable prospect. After all, one would by far prefer to commit the requisite talent and resources to addressing *their* systems. And yet as Germany's experience with Enigma amply demonstrated in the Second World War, this naturally favored approach can be an invitation to disaster.

The leakage—let alone interception—of confidential reports can frustrate the aims of the enterprise. To be sure, one occasionally successful pathway to report secrecy is to hide a message in open view, placed inconspicuously amid a mass of otherwise irrelevant matter. But this is perhaps too laborious and cumbersome for common employment.

This is not the place for debating the pros and cons of secrecy. But it can be taken as a given that in situations of competition and conflict of the sort at use with warfare and diplomatic relevancy, it is generally counterproductive to give the opponent a view of the cards of one's own hand. And when confidentiality is of the essence such measures as covert transmission and encryption are employed. However, when secrecy and security are matters of concern, the variety and volume of information reporting must be carefully limited to minimize the risk of interception. A difficult trade-off is at issue here that pits the volume of information transmission against its security.

Maintaining the security of confidential transmissions is one of reporting's most challenging demands. Nations spend vast fortunes on the pursuit of this objective, and it is seldom enough. Few human projects were ever subject to such tight security measures as the American atomic bomb project at Los Alamos. And yet it was totally precluded by Soviet espionage to the extent that their first atomic weapon was an exact replica to ours, down to the last nut and bolt.[14]

The reality of it is that communications security is almost a contradiction in terms. And the best way to ensure the security of one's own communications is to deploy against them the same level of expertise, effort, and cunning that one can expect of the opposition. While this is neither convenient nor inexpensive—and indeed but rarely attempted—it is critical whenever rigorous confidentiality is of the essence.

CHAPTER 5
RECEPTION

RECEIVING REPORTS

Reportage is a purposive enterprise aimed at providing useful information—material that recipients can utilize in the service of their interests, both cognitive and operationally practical. Accordingly, with reports it is, or should be, the intended recipient that is in the driver's seat: it is the recipient's needs that are paramount and whose interests predominate. The very expression of "reporting to someone" indicates functional subordination. Accordingly, the issue of what is of use or at least of interest to the recipient should never be far from a reporter's mind.

The reception of reports has two main components: collection and collation. Like a book newly obtained by a library, it has to be unpacked and duly affiliated to its mates—stored, cataloged, and rendered accessible where needed for further examination and reference. Basically three things can be done with a report once it arrives: it can be dismissed and discarded; it can be passed on to others; it can be acted upon in some reactive implementation; or finally, it can be stored for future utilization along with others. It is up to the recipient to decide which response is appropriate. And it is up to the sender to provide the recipient with suitable guidance in this process.

With reports there is a difference between receiving the mere communication itself and the message that it conveys. If the report is received in a language one does not understand (classically, Navajo) or in a code that one cannot unravel, its mere receipt is not of much avail: one does not access the message that constitutes its content. Even as it is one thing to *hear* what is said and another to *understand* it, so it is one thing to receive a message that conveys a report and another to receive that report itself. It is generally the latter that is at issue when one speaks unqualifiedly of report reception. Moreover, it is one thing to *consider* a report—to find it in one's in-box and take it up for consideration—and yet quite another thing to *accept* it through giving credence to what it purports and taking its content seriously. Reports often meet with the unhappy fate of being not just ignored, which is bad enough, but even being dismissed, which is positively ignominious.

In the absence of case-specific counterindications, report recipients are generally well advised to accept what they are told. For proceeding this way is generally cost effective vis-à-vis one's informational aims and purposes. If playing safe were all that mattered, one might well suspend judgment indefinitely. But it is simply not sensible to do so, since safety is not all. We adopt the policy of trust in the first instance because it is the most promising avenue toward our goals, and then we persist in it because we subsequently find not that it is unfailingly successful but that it is highly cost effective.[1] Information management based on principles of cooperation is a process of mutual benefit—for everyone is advantaged by adopting a mode of operation that maintains the best available balance of costs and benefits in this matter of creating a productively usable pool of information.

Above all, the attitude of the recipient toward the message of an intelligence report is a critical factor. No potential recipient is so deaf to a report as someone intent upon not hearing it. Despite a myriad of signals, Washington apparently did not realize in late 1941—or at any rate did not wish to acknowledge—that its insistence on an oil embargo was in effect tantamount to a declaration of war on Japan. In private and official matters alike, people have a natural tendency to view with skepticism anything that, if true, would have highly unwelcome implications.

The acceptance of a report is often helped or hindered by factors above and beyond its substantive content. The reportee's specific situation is an important determinative factor. George Kennan was very fortunate that his famous "Long Telegram" regarding Soviet policy reached Washington's policy marked at an unusually favorable and receptive moment and evoked a favorable response.[2] In the Second World War, both Stalin and FDR each worried that the other partner might arrange terms with Nazi Germany and leave the other in the lurch. In both cases there was ample evidence that this was not about to happen. But had any report—on either side—even hinted otherwise, it would have fallen on willing ears. A report is particularly appreciated when its message reinforces the cognitive and attitudinal predispositions of its recipients.

In the late stages of the Second World War, U.S. authorities rebuffed all reports of German willingness to capitulate following a destruction of Nazism by internal resistance forces. As one historian puts: "The very existence of an anti-Nazi group within Germany became a cause of embarrassment for the Roosevelt administration."[3] Many reports convey information that, in the well-worn phrase, "one just doesn't want to know."[4]

Sometimes too much information can also be a bad thing. The Allies learned after the war that around 250 reports in the German Admiralty archives dealt with the time and place of the cross-channel invasion. Only one was accurate, but the envisioning haystack effectively concealed this needle.[5]

A report is *rejected* when one endorses its denial; it is *declined* when one suspends judgment. This important distinction is often insufficiently heeded in the epistemology of information processing. For in-line with this distinction are two reactions to the reliability of sources. They can be deemed untrustworthy in the sense that one systemically declines acceptance of their claims and suspends judgment about them. Or they can be deemed deceptive in that one inclines to reject their reports and accept the contrary of what they claim. In the former case we treat our sources with unbelief, in the latter with disbelief. When we have lost confidence in the competence of a source, we refrain from accepting its reports. When we actually distrust the source—when we think it has become corrupted or even "turned"—then we will outright disbelieve its claims. (Note that the second situation is actually more informative: it obliquely provides us with information in hand, whereas the former leaves a blank. It's being reported by a deceptive source affects our judgment of the *probability* of the truth of what is reported, by way of decreasing it.)

When are we going to accept a claim to supposed fact and add it to the stock of our beliefs—our putative knowledge? This is obviously an issue that engages both theoreticians and laypeople. Philosophers incline favorably to Bishop Butler's idea that probability is the guide of life. Probability, in the sense of harmonization with the body of already available knowledge, is seen as the pivot. Accordingly, these theorists base their proceeding on the substantiating evidence that speaks for the substantive content of a claim.

However, in actual practice, it is generally needful have recourse to another line of consideration; namely, source reliability. In many cases we ourselves simply do not possess enough information or sufficient expertise to make an informed judgment on such matters and are largely or wholly dependent on the reliability of a reporting informant. In these circumstances our acceptance of a report will depend not on our evaluation of its substance but on our evaluation of its source.

If the source is deemed reliable we will accept what it claims; if not, then not.

But what is to be the threshold of acceptance—how much substantiation is to be required for a reported message to be deemed worthy of acceptance and implementation? The answer is that it all depends on the mode, manner, and purport of the utilization that is envisioned. The potential utility of its implementation in point of its potential for positive and negative results is the crux. For sure, when the risk is great, it is only sensible to require that the extent of substantiation is suitably great as well. Setting the threshold too high will proliferate errors of omission by leading to the inclusion of errors of commission. All one can hope to do is to set that threshold at a producing intermediation. It will not be possible to eliminate crisis altogether. But it should be possible to reduce its extent to a manageable minimum.

All the same, problems will arise in this context if the report at issue emanates from a source we deem to be highly reliable but is substantively doubtful on the basis of the information we otherwise have on the topic. When source reliability conflicts with report improbability we are invariably perplexed. When the reverse is the case there is, of course, no problem: the report is simply ignored.

The fact that the credence-acceptability of reports depends crucially on the recipient's trust in the reporter becomes a particularly critical factor in intelligence operations. To do its job properly, a nation's intelligence service must develop contacts with its enemies. But it can be difficult to assess whether those contacts are made for purposes of information or for purposes of betrayal. It becomes essential for those who contact the enemy to retain trust by reporting the matter to their superiors in full and frank detail. And the personal touch undoubtedly helps. A report almost invariably gains a more positive reception when the reporter or transmitter is persona grata—someone one likes or thinks well of. The most critical task for any intelligence service that provides information to a nation's decision makers is to secure their trust and their confidence in its competence. This is seldom an easy task.[6]

Some reports merely announce results—the winner of a lottery, say, or of a Nobel Prize. From some recipients point of view, it will, of course, be a prime issue whether the information conveyed by the report is welcome or unwelcome—whether it presents good news, bad news, or matters of indifference. But this issue of welcome, however important in itself, is irrelevant for our present purposes, which address the epistemic rather that the affective aspect of reportage. The only caveat here is that there may be some natural tendency to give credence to portentous reports of a markedly favorable or unfavorable coloration.

Even when reporting is done at the behest and on instructions of a reportee, the actual conduct of the enterprise often does not conform itself to this reportee's requirements. Thus intelligence operating field agencies are notoriously prone to report back to their control center the information they can conveniently obtain rather than information what is ardently being sought.[7] And this sort of proceeding can exact a big price. The loss of one single "small" item of information can lead to the unravelling of a big picture.

Consider the following reportorial set-up:

And now suppose that three sources inform us that the X is to be found in the position that is:

- Source 1: Not in the first row
- Source 2: Not in the third row
- Source 3: On one of the main diagonals

We can of course now locate X exactly at the center. But with any item lost—even the rather uninformative claim of Source 3—our ability to locate X is lost. The message of a report is often a puzzle that calls for assembling a complex and diversified cluster of pieces.

Be it true or not, acceptance of a report even by only a few can have enormous implications. Colonel Claus von Stauffenberg's bombing of Hitler's conference at the Wolf's Lair in East Prussia in July 1944 almost launched a successful military coup against the Nazi regime but for a handful of key people who accepted reports that Führer was yet well and in charge. The truth of a report is one thing; its status in the mind of a recipient quite another. And this makes mere rumor a powerful force on its own right.

RECIPIENTS

There are two classes of report recipients: *intended* recipients, to whom the report is specifically targeted, and *unintended* recipients, who get hold of it by one means or another. However, the intended recipients of a report need not be specifically identified by the sender and may in some instances not even exist as yet. Time capsules and cornerstone packets are clear instances of this circumstance.

Some untargeted reports are aimed indiscriminately at whoever chooses to attend to the matter. They are issued in the hope that some self-elected group will prove to be appreciative recipients of the report. Reports in reference works are a good example of this. Message bottles tossed into the sea and messages scratched into cell walls present analo-

TABLE 2. RECEPTION NEGATIVES AND THEIR CAUSES

Negativity	Sample Causative Etiology
One is disbelieved.	One speaks falsely too often (out of heedlessness or out of deceptiveness).
One is misunderstood.	One uses careless or inadequate formulations.
One is tuned out.	One speaks off the point (digresses) or speaks at undue length (even if it is to the point).

gously untargeted communications. In fact, the putative recipients of a report may have an even more speculative and mythic status—as when messages are sent by radio telescope "to whom it may concern" among the suppositional extraterrestrial life-forms imagined to be living on distant planets.[8]

Targeted reports, by contrast, are issued on the expectation that the information provided will be of interest and use to a specifically envisioned audience. And more often than not they are sent in the expectation that there will be no untargeted recipients at all—an expectation that often fails to be met. Thus the reports that Lieutenant General Hiroshi Ōshima, Japan's ambassador in Berlin sent to Tokyo regarding Germany's military potential and plans, found a more interested and attentive readership in Washington than in his foreign ministry at home.[9]

The identification of intended reportees can cause problems for a reporter. Thus with their massive ventures into individual behavior, governmental security agencies confront substantial administrative difficulties in this regard. To whom should an organization like the

FBI, the IRS, or the intelligence agencies pass on what sort of information. A plethora of legal and political problems pervade this entire terrain.

The senior managers of a large organization will receive reports through many delivery systems: colleague conversations, telephone calls, on-screen messages, and so on. Some scheduling and prioritizing is necessary for managing all this. Experience is a great guide here, but virtually any system is better than no system at all.

Effective communication requires proper cost-benefit coordination. It is governed by such principles as:

- Be sufficiently cautious in your claims to protect your credibility, but do not say so little that you become dismissed as a useless source.
- Formulate your statements fully and carefully enough so as to avoid misunderstanding but not with so much detail and precision as to weary your auditors and get tuned out.
- Make your message long (explicit, detailed, etc.) enough to convey your points but short enough to avert wasting the recipient's time, effort, and patience.
- Be sufficiently redundant so that a recipient who is not intensely attentive can still get the point but not so redundant as to bore or annoy or insult your auditors.
- Keep to the point but not so narrowly that your message is impoverished by lack of context.

All of these principles are fundamentally economic principles of balance; they all turn on finding a point after which the benefit of further gain in information falls below the cost demanded for its process of acquisition.

The reception of a report calls for an investment of attention, time, and energy, and a recipient is prepared to do this because he or she has or takes an interest in the matter. The extent to which a report bears information to these concerns of the recipient is, for the recipient, one of the key determinants of its value. Ideally, reporting should be client-oriented; it should focus on issues that are important for the recipient. But distraction is a major obstacle, for here it is not that the report fails to be received but that when it is the recipient's attention is oriented elsewhere.

This situation can and is often exploited by those who wish to have a report overlooked in creating useful distractions. Prior to the Allied cross-channel invasion of Normandy, elaborate measures were taken to create an illusionary army group in East Anglia under General George S. Patton through measures designed to fool aerial reconnaissance and communications monitoring alike. The idea was to create the impression of an impending assault across the Pas-de-Calais, thereby deflecting attention from the actual invasion site, Normandy.

ORGANIZATIONAL ASPECTS

Reportage within organizations mirrors the subordination relationships depicted in a hierarchical table of organization (TOE), with lower-level functionaries "reporting to" the superior who is their "boss." Subordination is reflected in the fact that one individual or unit "reports to" another. And there is no more ready way of gaining insight into an organization than via the reportage that flow along the connecting lines of its table of organization. Reporting here tracks the channels of power and control. The substantial resources that all nations dedicate to monitoring the supposedly confidential reports of others is a clear indication of the importance of reportage in human affairs. Nowadays if one power wants to send a message to another in a way that ensures attention, it will do well to send the communication to a third party by means that are sure to be intercepted by the intelligence service of the actually intended recipient.

Many organizations maintain logs for incurring reports to enable the future settlement of "What did they know and when did they know it?" issues. In this context many reports are made "for the record," as is the case with the regulation of deeds to record real estate transactions. The flow of power through the links of the organizational clout of an enterprise is one of its most critical features.

In most organizations there is an excess of reporting, with far more reports jostling about the system than is either necessary or desirable, resulting in a great deal of time and money being spent needlessly in dealing with reports. And such over-reporting poses special dangers in an organization whose functioning control over information is important. For with too much information astir and too many people given access, the due maintenance of control—let alone confidentiality—becomes effectively impossible.

CONFIDENTIALITY ISSUES AGAIN

The task of any security service is to protect secrets—to prevent reportage of information that can guide an opponent in pursuit of their objectives. But when unintended receipt cannot be blocked—as is all too generally the case—the next best procedure is to undermine confidence in its correctness by throwing doubt in the accuracy of the sources or the reliability of the reporters. Even when report reception cannot be blocked, report acceptance can be impeded.

When reportage patterns change this circumstance by itself "sends a message." In international dealings changing the code used for one's own communication is a noteworthy step: Has one's prior code become compromised? Are hostile initiatives being contemplated? Are internal power arrangements in process of revision? We have a red flag indicating that one way or another something of wider significance is in progress.

Report recipients generally tend to give greater credence to reports that they are not intended to receive; since, in order to maintain their credibility, sources are unlikely to deceive the intended recipients of these reports. In espionage, in particular, intercepting the private communications of one's opponents carries an assurance only rarely matched by the information they disseminate for general consumption.

The reading of reports by nonintended eyes makes a bad situation even worse. Unless they have carrier pigeons at their disposal, the defenders of a besieged city may not want to send out the message that they are running out of food or ammunition. A vivid example of a failure of military operations owing to compromised secrecy was the Allied raid on the German-occupied French port of Dieppe in 1942. Intended as a dress rehearsal for later cross-channel operations, it ended in disaster owing to poor planning security management.[10]

Maintaining due confidentiality sometimes requires measures offensive not just to one's enemies but also to one's allies. Japan gave Nazi Germany no advance notice of inaugurating hostilities with the United States, even as Germany had given Japan no notice of attacking Russia.[11]

Alike with individuals and organizations, it is often important to control access to information used and thus to target reports to particular intended recipients to the exclusion of others. Especially with military matters and issues of national security, it becomes important to compartmentalize operational information and tightly restrict access. Alike in matters of business, criminality, and national security, some information is transmitted on the basis of being "super-secret," "recipient's eyes only," "burn after reading," and so on. "Need to know" becomes a crucial principle. This opens up a whole host of "official secret" confidentiality and right-to-access problems. And at the forefront here stands the virtually universal redundancy of overestimating the security of one's own communication.[12]

The issue of confidentiality arises whenever reports are intended to reach only one particular limited group of authorized recipients. The problems posed by the security of information are enormously ramified and complex—especially in an era where information is not stored on paper but floats about in cyberspace.

Breaking into an opponent's mailbox of secrets—monitoring his communications—is invaluable in conflict situations, but it is seldom decisive. For the information that it yields relates only to plans and projects and only rarely reflect reality since, as the poet has it, "The best laid plans of mice and men gang aft agley." Granted, it helps enormously to read the enemy's mind. But wars are not won by mind readers. All the same, if we are engaged in strongly interactive enterprises, it will be very useful to me to read the reports that come to or emanate from you. Every national security service in the world that is worth its salt spies on its friends as well as its enemies.

RECEPTION NEGATIVITIES

As already noted, when one endeavors to convey information to someone, various sorts of unpleasant reactions can occur. One seldom receives heartfelt thanks for reporting unwelcome news. And here arises the problem of outright resistance, creating a certain tension, because the reporter has no choice but to report on what sources render available.[13]

Reports, of course, can convey both good and bad news—messages that are welcome and messages that are decidedly unwelcome. There are things the reportee simply does not want to hear. FDR and his advisors found extensive and credible reports of the Soviet massacre of Political officers in the Katyn Forest, a highly inconvenient obstacle to supportive relations with an essential ally, and simply clamped a lid on the whole matter. A reporter is well advised to take this into account—in particular by taking steps to formulate unwelcome news in credible terms. Indeed, the reporter may well refrain from sending highly unwelcome reports of very low credibility.

One has to distinguish between the *reaction* evoked by a report and the *response* that a recipient makes to it. The *reaction* is something that is affectively evaluative in nature and proceeds along a spectrum ranging from the negative (dislike or dismay) to a welcoming positivity. People generally have this sort of reaction to novel information, viewing it as good or bad news. But only a very few reports evoke a *response* from the recipient by way of inducing them to do something about it. Most of the time reports, welcome or not, are such that there is nothing we can do about it.

When a major defeat is suffered by the armed forces of a country, its intelligence service is apt to be the first to know about it, thanks to monitoring the inner communications and public broadcasts of a rejoicing enemy. But they are decidedly disinclined to pass the word to the home leadership, knowing full well that the message is likely to become tarred with the negativity of the message. When General Friedrich von Paulus surrendered his Sixth Army at Stalingrad, senior German officials vied with each other to not be the one who informed the Führer, rightly anticipating the rage that would be evoked by such grievous news.

One significant source of error in interpreting reports is the tendency to dismiss possibilities whose probably is deemed to be low. It is easy to forget that, as with a roulette wheel, the entire spectrum of possibility may well be an aggregate of how-probability developments. (After all, one or another of these outcomes will have to be realized.) This phenomenon is particularly ominous on military and diplomatic intelligence deliberations. An adequately founded intelligence center would always do well to have a "devil's advocate"–style warrior to ask both whether situations relegated to negotiable probability status are properly being characterized as such and whether in the circumstances they can really be ruled out altogether.

RECEPTION ATTITUDE EXAMPLES: CHURCHILL, ROOSEVELT, AND HITLER

It is interesting to contrast the different ways in which key leaders in the Second World War reacted to signals intelligence regarding the enemy's moves on the stage of international politics and diplomacy.

Reports run the risk of being dismissed out of hand when they conflict with well-entrenched preconceptions. As the French say, *il n'y a personne de si aveugle que celui qui ne veut pas voir.* Douglas MacArthur himself acknowledged that at the outbreak of the Korean war, "we refused to believe what our intelligence told us was in fact happening because it was at variance with the prevailing climate of opinion in Washington and Tokyo."[14]

A closed mind is beyond the reach of reportage: "On one occasion, when Walther Seifert, chief of the Evaluation Bureau of the cryptographic service (*Forschungsamt*) of the Germany Foreign Office, forwarded to Hitler a report with unwelcome news, an adjunct objected: 'How can you submit such a report to the Führer at this time?'. . . When the Führer has made a decision, we must no longer disturb his intention."[15] At one point when intelligence chief Reinhard Gehlen's figures on Russian troop strength were submitted to Hitler, the Führer protested that they were "total idiocy" and that its sender should be committed to an insane asylum.[16]

Churchill took a close and lively interest in intelligence material, eagerly reading his daily quota of reports and anxiously ensuring that his subordinates made good use of them. He had "an intense interest in and curiosity about everything which contributed to the nation's war effort" and "found satisfaction on exploring each of them, great and small."[17] It impressed all concerned that he never overruled his chiefs of staff whenever they presented an agreed recommendation.

Franklin D. Roosevelt's approach to intelligence reports has been described in the following terms.

> Roosevelt and his diplomatic advisers, buffeted by political necessity, assured by personal conviction or intuition, or constrained by the paucity of viable alternatives, seemingly disregarded the signal-intelligence evidence when determining a policy. In 1941 the White House and the State Department clung to the hope that economic sanctions would restrain Japan even though Japanese intercepts clearly indicated that Tokyo would not be deterred by embargoes. After Germany's invasion of the Soviet Union, Roosevelt was not deterred from committing American supplies to Russia by signals intelligence (largely Japanese) indicating that the Soviets would quickly succumb to German attack. The specter of a separate peace between a beleaguered Soviet Union and a triumphant Germany haunted American deliberations over a second front, despite consistent evidence from the decrypts that neither Berlin nor Moscow had any interest in a separate peace.

At the White House the president's naval aide delivered classified naval documents twice a day, including the diplomatic decrypts. The president displayed a curious insouciance toward the signals intelligence. He frequently did not bother to read, let alone study, the decrypts. The morning briefing often took place in the presidential bathroom, where the aide would close the toilet lid, sit on it, and read aloud the foreign messages as the president shaved. In the afternoons the venue switched to an anteroom off the White House Map Room, where Roosevelt was content to listen to the oral report while he had his polio-wasted legs massaged or his troublesome sinuses packed by the White House physician. The president did not retain any decrypts for study or future reference.[18]

With regard to FDR, one recent analysis of the situation arrives at the following conclusion:

Franklin Roosevelt reserved for himself all important foreign policy decisions and was supremely confident of his ability to understand the international scene and his country's place in it. His approach to foreign affairs depended more on intuition than on information, and his posture toward certain countries (e.g., China and France) or issues (decolonization) was as likely to reflect personal biases as professional briefings. . . . When he wanted information, he tended to avoid formal intelligence channels, preferring instead to canvass indiscriminately the opinion of official and private visitors to the White House, some of whom had no more claim to his attention than an old school tie or a social relationship. His idiosyncratic decision-making style, with its reliance on personality and intuition and its abhorrence of system, made him a poor customer for the information services. One student of the president's attitude toward intelligence has noted: "He much preferred his own wide range of contacts—inside and outside government—from whom he gleaned bits and pieces of information. From these, and from his own instincts and preference, FDR arrived at conclusions that were often at variance with intelligence analysis."[19]

The approach to intelligence closely mirrored the management style of these war leaders. Roosevelt's approach to intelligence was decidedly cavalier. He addressed only large issues of international politics and left warfare to the professionals. Stalin was guided almost entirely by his political preconceptions. Hitler often descended from these higher levels to micromanage even tactical arrangements.[20] And he tended to trust the reports of agents and unconventional sources rather more than the technically sophisticated information provided by informed experts.[21] Churchill took a close interest in intelligence matters but left their complementation to the professionals. There could be no clearer illustration of the fact that the ultimate value of reports hinges on the attitude of the reportee.[22]

CHAPTER 6
COGNITIVE IMPORTANCE

REPORT IMPORTANCE

Their importance is clearly a crucial feature of reports. For one thing, importance is—or should be—our indispensable guide to the rationality of resource allocation. There is no point in devoting time and effort to trivia. It is not just inefficient but outright irrational to allocate to unimportant matters resources that can and should be dedicated to more important ones.

A recipient will, of course, welcome reports that are not only accurate but also informative: correctness is not compensatory for negligible significance and utility. Importance is paramount: it is in everyone's interest—reporter and reportee alike—that reports should provide important information.

The importance of reports has two principal dimensions: importance for informative understanding and importance for productive application—theoretical and practical importance, as it were. This chapter will focus on the former issue.

A dictionary will define importance somewhat as follows: "having great significance, weight, consequence, or value." And it will go on to list such synonyms as significance, essentiality, and moment and such antonyms as insignificance, inessentiality, and negligibility. The important things are clearly those that count and the unimportant ones those that don't. But how is the score to be kept?

The cognitive importance of reports is best assessed by "the experts," the people who have the widest and deepest knowledge of the relevant domain. But their practical importance is best determined by the intended recipients themselves in relation to their agenda. It has to be realized, too, that the monitoring of reports has only limited utility in matters of practice and action. For people's actions are determined by what they *think*, and their reportings are merely indicative of what they *say*.[1] It takes a considerable knowledge to implement this abstractions effectively.

The importance of a report can differ drastically for different and differently situated recipients. To one it may convey something already well known, while to another it is merely "old news." One recipient may be unable to do anything whatever about the information it conveys, while for another recipient it issues a clarion call for dramatic action. Importance is something relative to the recipient. Strictly speaking one should not talk of the importance of a report but rather of its importance for certain recipients—that is, those who have "a need to know." Importance becomes universal and unqualified only when everyone is involved.[2]

One major indicator of the importance of a report is its impact upon the recipient's plan of action. For while we humans live in the present, we inwardly act with a view to the situation of the future: we do things *now* to determine or influence the conditions of things *there*. That is to say, we make plans, and these depend on the information that comes to be at our disposal in reports. Those reports that change our outlook in ways that call for a change in our planning are the ones to which we do and must attach substantial importance.

To be sure, people have of late taken in droves to reporting their quotidian activities via social media, acting on the counterintuitive principle that to be noticed for foolishness is better than not being noticed at all. However, *de minimis non curat lex*—and indeed not only does the law not trouble much about trifles but neither should the rest of us. Importance is not, however, the sole consideration, because its significance is tempered by the question of the likelihood of achieving an effective resolution of the problem at issue with the means currently at one's disposal. Obviously, no matter how important a question may be, if there is virtually no chance of securing an adequate answer by the means and methods actually at one's disposal, then the inquiry is pretty much pointless.

All the same, a significant aspect of a report's importance arises from its synergetic interaction with others. When one report makes possible the location of a ship at sea along one line of orientation and a second report places it along another, their combination possibilizes a precise fix. Reports that seem uninformative and unimportant individually and by themselves may function as parts of a group that has transcendent importance in its coordinated collectivity. With reports the whole may have a value far greater than the sum of the parts.

What is unquestionably the biggest problem in regard to the importance of reported information is that this is all too often something that emerges only in distant retrospect with the wisdom of hindsight. Initially, reports may convey on a minuscule hint—the first small wind-gust that precedes a variable hurricane. And even these minor foreshadowings may be almost undetectable in the multitudinous environment of other, more prominent and seemingly more significant developments. In the ordinary course of things there is generally no practicable way to distinguish between the foreshadowings of portentous developments and the run of the mill eventuations that invariably surround it.

Sometimes reports are notable for their absence. For one thing the non-arrival of expected reports is always a troubling circumstance indicating that something is amiss. Thus, when a spy is captured his captor will often take care, when possible, to continue his home reportage in the usual way, albeit now with misinformation in place of significant intelligence.

Occasionally, there are black holes in reportage, regions from which effectively no reports whatever emanate. This leads to a response of deep, dark suspicions. Reportage, like nature, abhors a vacuum, so that information voids readily become filled with wild conjecture.

ASSESSING REPORT IMPORTANCE

Cognitive importance accordingly is an index of the extent to which one thing deserves more attention (time, effort, energy) than another. The crucial thing here is inherent in the question of how prominent a place in the sun a report deserves. One aspect of the matter can be viewed in light of the idea of a perfected information manual for the domain at issue. And importance will here be reflected in space allocation.

The cognitive importance of the information conveyed in a report will hinge on matter of the extent of its alteration in the preexisting state of knowledge. Does it add little to what is already known or does it add a great deal? Or does it subtract by undermining ideas in which one once had confidence? Does it perhaps have cataclysmic implications and enjoin on to "go back to the old drawing board" and rethink the entire matter. To what extent is it an essential feature for the manifold of our understanding? How radical a change would its absence make? In our account of the relevant issues, would we have to rewrite a single sentence or a paragraph or a chapter or perhaps even the whole book? The pivot is the issue of how large a place a contention deserves to have on the register of what we take to be our knowledge. To say that one fact or finding is more important than another is to make a judgment of worth or value. Accordingly, it merits a greater expenditure of intellectual resources—of attention, concern, time, and effort to discover, learn, explain, and teach the item at issue. Importance, that is to say, is a fundamentally economic concept—one of the pivotal concepts of the rational economy of cognition.

By contrast, the practical importance of a report pivots on the question: What is to be done about it? And here two further issues arise: What is the direction, scale, and extent of the appropriate reaction? And what is the imminence and urgency of the responsive agency? Clearly, if a great deal needs to be done right way, the report is of paramount practical importance. However, the practical importance of a report depends upon how useful the information that it provides is for meeting people's needs and wants, aims and goals, purposes and objectives. It becomes supreme when their very survival is at stake.

The cognitive importance of a report turns on how substantial a revision in our body of relevant beliefs is wrought by our accepting it; that is, the extent to which its endorsement would cause geological tremors reverberating across the cognitive landscape. But two very different sorts of things can be at issue here: either a mere *expansion* of our knowledge by additions or, more seriously, a *revision* of it that involves *replacing* some of its members and readjusting the remainder so as to restore overall consistency. This second sort of change in a body of knowledge, its *revision* rather than mere *augmentation*, is, in general, the more significant matter, and a report is of greater import when it forces revisions rather than merely fills in some part of the terra incognita of knowledge. And so what we have to deal with here is an essentially seismological standard of importance. It is based on the question, If the contention or thesis at issue were abrogated or abandoned, how large would the ramifications and implications of this circumstance be? How extensive would be the shocks and tremors reverberating throughout the whole range of what we (presumably) know?

In general, the more reports on any given topic are astir, the smaller the proportion of important ones. Think in this context of working a crossword puzzle. Here two distinct sorts of significant contributions are possible. There are those that help to fill in more spaces—to get a fuller account of things—and then there are those that destabilize a preexisting picture and constrain us to rethink and rework our view of things. And it is the latter that are particularly important. For here— and throughout the cognitive domain—our paramount concern is not just to get answers to our questions but answers that fit together overall, forming a structure that is not just large but solid.

Cognitive importance is not coordinate with the sheer volume of information. For quantity itself possesses a danger in reporting. For it can serve to conceal the meaningful needles in a haystack of insignificant detail. The emergence of the Internet has transformed reporting in many ways—especially in regard to the unending range of personal opinion on information. We here once more confront the rule that quantity and quality stand in a teeter-totter relationship of competing complementarity where more of the one yields less of the other. Most significant report items come with a penumbra of insignificant ones. And in general the information product in mass reporting is subject to a principle of diminishing returns: as the number of reports grows larger, the proportion of really significant information declines. For the watchword here is quality not quantity. What we are after is knowledge and understanding. And there is a good reason to think that knowledge answers not with the *volume* of information—its sheer amount—but only with its logarithm.[3] This difference must be borne in mind with reporting, whose object is—or should be—to focus not just on information detail but on the crème de la crème.

Predictive reports raise special issues of concern since prediction regarding future developments constitutes a category of special interest. Three factors are of prime significance here: *imminence* (in point of futurity), *significance* (in point of import), and *likelihood* (in point of probability of realization). Each of these factors can be classified as low, middling, and high. Obviously, when all three rate high, the report is of paramount importance. It is the mixed bag sort of report (imminence—middling; probability—low; significance—high) that will be the most difficult and vexatious to deal with.

IS IMPORTANCE OBJECTIVE?
COGNITIVE IMPORTANCE VS. INTEREST

The extent to which a report is cognitively important can in general be assessed and evaluated along a scale of small, medium, large. The grading importance is not a thing of arbitrary subjectivity: it is an objective matter governed by impersonal norms. The cognitive importance of a report lies in the contribution it makes to this preestablished knowledge—and this is something about which a recipient may well be mistaken. Its practical importance is a function of what a recipient *should* do about it by the rational rights of the matter, and may thus not be anything like what is actually done. Importance, be it cognitive or practical, is a matter subject to rational nous and does not lie substantively in the eyes of the recipient but rather objectively in the nature of their situation. Seeming importance is not necessarily the real thing. For while seeming importance lies in the eyes of the beholder, actual importance does not. Something can be very important for someone of which they know nothing. People may be totally oblivious to developments like disasters or windfalls, which are of paramount importance for them.

The contrast between importance and interest is yet another reminder that there is a crucial difference between relativism and contextualism. Something is a matter of *indifferentist relativism* when it lies subjectively "in the eyes of the beholder" as it were—when it is simply up to the individual to effect an otherwise unfettered choice one way or the other.

Hindsight often reveals that *apparent* importance—importance as we judge it here and now—is something decidedly different from *real* importance; that is, importance as it will eventually emerge to view with the accession of further and fuller information. In the early 1940s, American security authorities deemed it important to monitor the mails from the United States to Germany and took elaborate measures to intercept and censor. In retrospect this can be seen as a massive exercise in ineffectual effort since merely announcing this was being done would have deflected any illicit communications into other more vulnerable lines.

The value of reports is situational: it pivots on people's requirements and needs. So it must be stressed that while the cognitive importance of reports is indeed an *objective* factor, it is nevertheless *contextual* in nature. For it does critically depend on how the arriving information fits into the wider manifold of what it is that is already in place. Even as it is foolish to think that what you don't know can't hurt you, so it is comparably foolish to think that something people do not deem important is for this very reason not so. Recall here the biblical admonition, "If the householder had known when the thief was coming, he would not have left the house unprotected" (Luke 12:39).

Cognitive importance is a matter of comparative utility for understanding, explaining, and predicting matters regarding the issue at hand. And this need bear no fixed relation to the extent to which people find them to be interesting.[4] Interest is something else again. It differs from importance in being predominantly personal and subjective; it lies largely in the eyes of the beholder. Matters that are quite interesting need not be of much importance—and the reverse can also be so. But importance is something that inheres in the nature of things rather than in our thoughts. An extremely interesting subject can be relatively unimportant in the larger scheme of things. (The prominence of sporting competitions or games like chess or contract bridge, for example, shows that things can be extremely interesting to people without being very important in themselves.) And in this light the difference between something being important for someone and its seeming important to this individual is not only real but crucial. People not uncommonly assign to an issue an importance it does not deserve and the reverse is true as well.

CHAPTER 7
INTERPRETATION PROBLEMS

WHY INTERPRETATION?

In matters of diplomatic and military intelligence, the reports at one's disposal are all too often altogether insufficient to answer one's questions. The partial information they provide will—as in a crossword puzzle—provide *some* relevant data, but they are often interrogatively insufficient. And the situation can be even worse. For we generally do not know just what it is that we don't know. With a crossword puzzle we have a clear view of the extent of our ignorance and the situation of its relationship to what is known. But in actual fact this is generally not the case. And ignorance about the extent and nature of our ignorance renders us blind even to the questions that matter for us—let alone the answers to them.

All this means that understanding reports calls for interpretation that goes well beyond the overtly specified information. For what a report says is one thing, and what it means is another. It is far from sufficient for the effective utilization of reports that they be received and noted. They must be *interpreted* as well. And this requires technical resources that are often not available to the recipient and establishes a need for advisers, consultants, and expert counselors.

One seasoned intelligence manger has put it well: "The generally accepted view that it is the duty of the Intelligence officer to 'give just the facts, please' has little relevance in a modern governmental structure. In the first place, the facts are often such that the policy-makers are unable interpret them without expert advice. Secondly, and obviously, the choice of facts is critical, and the Intelligence officer's decision as to which facts are relevant and which should be presented to the policy-makers is often the major initial step in the decision process."[1]

Prior to the utilization and implementation of reports, three processes are conjointly required: accession, translation/content-determination, and interpretation, dealing respectively with what the reports is, what is says, and what it means. In exploiting reports, all three of these are in intermittently interactive symbioses: there is a close interrelationship between detailing the report's own message and contextualizing it within the wider environment of relevant others. In the Second World War it was characteristic to British practice at Bletchley's handling of Germany intercepted radio messages to allocate preparation and interpretation to the same functionaries—to the great benefit of report exploitation. To the regret of many—and unquestionably also to the detriment of the enterprise—American practice then and later departed from this beneficial model. For reasons of turf protection the interception and preparation of reports (via the NSA) and their collection and interpretation (via the CIA) became separated in a manner that, to the mind of most impartial observers, significantly compromises the adequacy of the overall processes.[2]

The critical task—and key problem—in interpreting reports is fitting a newly achieved report into the framework of already available information. As long as the report is not redundant and reconfirmatory, two other prime prospects arise at this point: (1) the report *augments* the information one already has or (2) the report *contradicts* what one already knows—it simply does not jibe and imposes the stark choice between simply rejecting the report and revising the preexisting body of information so as to make room for it. This issue of revision and accommodation is one of the most difficult and challenging tasks of information processing.

In practice this process of best-fit determination and information harmonization is generally left to the interactive apprehension of informed minds. In these matters considerations of general principle do not go very far. Interpretation requires for contextualization within a large manifold of relevant information. As one knowledgeable discussant put it in terms of the Second World War intelligence: "The full meaning of the information conveyed by a message [intercepted in monitoring enemy communications] was only rarely self-evident from the translation alone, and it was usually necessary to draw out its significance by providing it with a context and setting it against a background as like as possible to that which would have been in the mind of the sender."[3]

Interpretation calls for contextualization within a large manifold of relevant information. As one knowledgeable discussant put it in discussing Second World War intelligence, "The full meaning of the information conveyed by a message [intercepted in monitoring enemy communications] was only rarely self-evident from the translation alone, and it was usually necessary to draw out its significance by providing it with a context and setting it against a background as like as possible to that which would have been in the mind of the sender."[4]

Contextualization is crucial in interpreting information. And in providing intelligence estimates, it is highly productive to specify explicitly the framework of background assumptions on which one's judgments are based.[5] Throughout the field of intelligence—be it military, diplomatic, or commercial—the link between reported activity and planned purpose, and thus between past and future, present a chasm that can be crossed only by sheer conjecture. Crossing this divide in a credible way calls for extensive contextual knowledge and superior acumen. In this context competent interpretations are worth their weight in gold.

Often, too, the reporting deals with its issues in a disjointed way, with some relevant information arriving from different sources at different times. But productive report interpretation cannot then be achieved in isolation; it demands reciprocal alignment and coordination with a larger context. Thus, consider the following set-up:

Source No. 1 reports that the *X* is in the first row; source No. 2 reports that it is not in a corner position. Between the two of them, they provide for an exact location—but only if they are duly combined.[6] Each report acquires a significance that is there only in the presence of the other.

The talent for ampliative reasoning—of drawing plausible conclusions from insufficiently informative premises—is a crucial asset for report interpretation The interpreter must be able to "connect the dots" and construct a meaningful picture from mere bits and pieces. Practice can help to develop this ability. And a deep knowledge of contextual matters is a necessary requirement here, but it is not sufficient. There has to be ingenuity and good judgment as well.

After all, reportage tells us what people *say* not what they *think*—to reemphasize an important point. Thus, in matters of military intelligence, there is the classic difficulty of weighing capability against intention: of estimating what an opponent is going to do with the forces and resources at their disposal. Given the modern technology of observation the former—capability—is readily determined. But intentions and plans are not so readily open to inspection. For this reason, monitoring an appropriate communication becomes a not less critical issue than monitoring an opponent's focus, and reports regarding the former are no less welcome to decision makers.[7]

The interpretation of reports requires their correlation, coordination, and systematization. Both internal detail and externally contextual harmony are essential requisites for such proceedings. The functional equivalent of memory and recollection are also required to provide resources for the effective interpretation of reports. If filing, indexing, and cross-referencing did not exist, report interpreters would have to invent them. Without the proper contextualization of a "paper trail," as it were, one would often be blind to the message of a report. With regard to the interception and decoding of enemy messages in the Second World War, one experienced commentator remarks that "the full meaning of the information conveyed by a message was only rarely self-evident from the translation alone, and it was usually necessary to draw out its significance by providing it with a context and setting it against a background as taken as possible to that which could have been in the minds of the . . . . sender and receiver."[8]

Ignorance may sometimes be bliss, but it is unlikely to be so in matters of report interpretation. Here knowledge is crucial—especially contextual knowledge.[9] For contextualization is an indispensable necessity in report interpretation, and one of the key difficulties in interpreting reports is lacking a firm idea of the limitation of one's information. Let it be that observers report that the enemy has just instituted food rationing in the areas along its defensive fortress. What does this mean? Have their crops failed? Has their transport system collapsed? Are they trying to show up particular features of "We're all suffering in this corner, even the people on the home front?" Does it foreshadow some sort of impending action? Only someone with extensive knowledge of prevailing conditions can decide the matter. Its meaning cannot be read off just from the report itself. Thus, if the report says that Y has replaced X as Ruritania's foreign minister, then given the respective training and past performance of these individuals this change may betoken major and far-reaching changes in that country's foreign policy. But this is something that can only be discerned by someone with an extensive knowledge of the contextual issues. In complex and important matters, it is only with the wisdom of eventual hindsight that one can tell the true significance of a report. All that can be done at the time is to make every practicable effort to contextualize it in its larger setting.[10]

And so, for meaningful interpretation one must reach out from beyond the report itself. As in working puzzles—crosswords for example—solving one piece often unlocks the door to dealing with others. Contextual information can prove vitally significant here. Thus suppose that we do not know whether the overall configuration at issue is as per I or as per II.

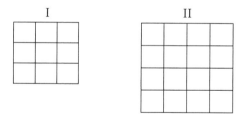

And suppose we are informed that the sought for position is:

- Report 1: Not in the first row.
- Report 2: Not in the third row.
- Report3: Not in the first column.
- Report 4: Not in the third column.

Then in the setting of case I, we can solve our location problem easily. But in case II, we remain at sea. And of course if we do not know how that positional framework is configured—if this situation falls into our "sphere of ignorance"—then our otherwise useful information can be useless. In these matters what you don't know can cause substantial harm.

The available reports often fall short when we need answers to our questions. And if that need is acute we are driven to guesswork—to supplementing what those reports actually provide by what they merely suggest. We thus fill an informative gap by plausible guesswork. And this invariably requires being well informed about peripheral matters. Random guesswork is worthless but well-informed, expert guesswork can be priceless.

And all too often, it is just this—the boundary between what we know and what we do not know—is what is the most difficult to establish. Knowing just what it is that one does not know is generally difficult and often impossible. And when reports are embraced in a penumbra of ignorance, it can be very difficult to make proper sense of them.

At this point some significant conceptual distinctions enter the picture. Not only is there the aforementioned difference between what a report *says* and what it *means* but also there is a significant difference between what something means *to* someone in terms of what they *actually do* with it and what it means *for* someone in terms of what they, properly speaking, *should do* with it if they managed matters correctly and appropriately. These two are of course not necessarily the same thing.

Report interpretation is contextualization. Moving beyond the text itself, this comes in two forms. First, there is *narrow* contextualization in the light of germane information that bears immediately on the issues of the message. And then there is *broad* contextualization in the light of a report's significance within the global context of relevant fact. The movement of a ship as part of a flotilla illustrates the former mode of contextualization; an impending seaborne invasion illustrates the latter.

However, there are many different pitfalls along the pathways to report interpretation, and they are especially prominent in matters of military and diplomatic intelligence. Prominent on the list are such issues as:

- flawed transmissions
- deceitful presentations (disinformation)
- slanted presentations
- imperfect translations
- misguided predispositions
- discordant contextualizations

It is little wonder that throughout recent history the agencies involved in the processing and interpretation of reports have seen an ever continuing enhancement in point of resources, status, and power.

However, alike in military and diplomatic affairs, those who have access to intelligence reports and are involved in its interpretation and implementation are often resented by other functionaries. One recent study describes the issue in terms of the following example: "[Until the First World War, the German officer corps] did not merely ignore intelligence, they fought it. For intelligence threatened their jobs. . . . Their knowledge gives [intelligence specialists] a certain power and . . . such power enables them to demand . . . access to the top [commanders]. And the existing officers resist this."[11] Reports are particularly problematic when they indicate a radical departure from a well-established normal course of things. Reports relating to an outbreak of hostilities under conditions of strategic surprise and "sneak attacks" vividly illustrate this circumstance.

In matters of reporting the extraordinary, there is an important distinction between the outlandish and the unusual—between reports that should be met with dismissive skepticism and those evoking mere surprise. Sightings of the Loch Ness monster or of UFOs fall into the former category. While there is nothing inherently absurd about this at the level of theoretical possibility, one has been down this particular road to nowhere so often that it is unproductive to report the trip. But merely unusual developments that are nonconforming outlaws on the axis of experience are something else again. Granted, the trip situations are not subject to a sharply marked boundary of differentiation. A perceptive judgment call is needed in these matters.

In early December 1941, Tokyo instructed the Japanese embassy in Washington, D.C., to burn its secret papers and to destroy its cryptographic machine. America's incredibly efficient intelligence apparatus intercepted and decoded this message and actually managed for it to reach America's secretary of state before the Japanese ambassador himself.[12] However, the significance of this report would have been lost to anyone who did not realize that the actions it indicated invariably presaged the outbreak of hostilities. When the top officials in Washington alerted their senior commanders overseas that an outbreak of war with Japan was imminent, they made no effort to contextualize this by a reminder that the Russo-Japanese War earlier in the century commenced with a surprise Japanese attack on the Russian fleet in its base at Port Arthur. In the light of this historical datum, the war warning acquires a more ominous significance. In matters of military and diplomatic intelligence, appropriate report interpretation calls for a grasp of a wide context of relevant knowledge on the interpreter's part. It often becomes necessary to call upon the diversified collaboration of multiple talents.

Seldom, if ever, is the information bearing a significant point of intelligence as complete as we would wish. As Carl von Clausewitz sagely put it, "We always know much less of the actual condition and of the designs of the enemy than we assume in forming our own plans." And this has obvious consequences, regarding which Clausewitz is once again right on target, "We cannot even imagine the full extent of the uncertainty [of our information] . . . and since we cannot obtain certainty, we must recognize that in war nothing can be carried out without a risk."[13]

Ironically, the information problem sometimes is the very reverse, rooting not in a dearth of data but rather in a surfeit. For example, "There were so many competing analyses of communist intentions doing the rounds in Washington [at the time of the Tet Offensive in Vietnam in 1967] that it was impossible to know which one was right."[14] Proper judgement in intelligence matters can arise as readily from a glut as from a dearth of information.

A key problem in the information culture of the present is identifying the important trees in the forest; that is, getting a clear view of the items that really matter, which of course calls for identifying those items in the first place. As one acute commentator has it, "In this climate the need for intelligence has changed. The difficulty of collecting the secrets has now become the challenge of *finding* the secrets among the mass of information pouring like a torrent past our nose. The difficulty is spotting the real facts we need and fishing them out as the flood pours by."[15] When the mass of available data is vast and ever-growing the issue becomes one of describing just what to ask of the information we have. And this questions-centered approach requires a deep understanding of the entire field at issue. It is not just a matter of having a field but deciding just where to dig our well, and it requires a knowledgeable prospector to get this right.

With report interpretation, experience has to be one's guide, There is, however, the monitory example of John Locke's story of the Siamese gentleman who dismissed as outlandish fable the report of a European visitor that the winter's cold solidified the water of rivers to a point where people could walk across them is instructive in this regard. In interpreting reports we have to fit them into the wider context of our own experience.

And not only should the interpreter be knowledgeable, but they should also be *objective* and able to maintain a clear distinction between what evidence indicates to be so in contrast to what one would like to have.

Text interpretation is a matter of conveying *what the report says*. This is impersonal: what is said is (or should be) the same for everyone—it should be reliable. But whatever can be interpreted can also be misinterpreted. Without trustworthy interpretation, recipients are left to their own resources, which may not be of the best. When Churchill forwarded to Stalin some of the telling reports indicating that Germany was on the verge of launching its Operation Barbarossa invasion of the Soviet Union, Stalin regarded this as misinformation intended by Britain to lure him into disagreement and discord with his good, newfound friend Adolf Hitler. Distrust of Britain ran too deep in Stalin's thinking to permit any other construal.

PLAUSIBILITY: FIT, CONSILIENCE, AND HARMONIZATION

A report can relate in the following three ways to its preexisting context:

- It can *agree* with it. (Of course, the greater the agreement, the less the news value—the more plausible but also redundant.)

- It can *disagree* with it. (Of course, the greater the disagreement the greater the news value—but also the apparent implausibility.)
- It can *supplement* it, by neither agreeing nor disagreeing but augmenting our relevant information.

Of course these various features can come in combination. Ideally, a report would come from a reliable source, have enough redundancy to provide plausibility, and provide a good deal of informative supplementation.

The conflict among reports is one of the biggest problems of report management. Thus, suppose for the sake of illustration that three sources of varying reliability report as follows:

- Report R1 from Source No. 1. The enemy sent three divisions to reinforce the five divisions holding sector A.
- Report R2 from Source No. 2. The enemy withdrew two divisions from the five holding sector A, but sent four replacements.
- Report R3 from Source No. 3. The enemy has made no change in his dispositions in sector A.

Suppose that we assess the initial credibility of these three reports as being, respectively: low, low, and middling. And now let it be that two questions are at issue:

(Q1) How many enemy divisions are in sector A?
(Q2) How many of these divisions are fresh replacements?

The answers to these questions provided by our sources run as follows:

	Q1	Q2
R1 (L)	8	3
R2 (L)	8	5
R3 (M)	6	0

Unfortunately, there is no straightforward and automatic way to resolve such conflicting reports and amalgamate them into an informative conclusion. The safest course would be to hedge the answer to Q1 by claiming 4 to 8 and Q2 by claiming 0 to 5. And if greater precisions were described, one might hazard the estimation of "about 7" for Q1 and "about 2" for Q2 (combining the two consistent week moves are one middling and then averaging things out). Yet the fact remains that in the face of conflicting reports the most and best one can do is to resort to cautiously managed guesswork. (Note that this simple example also illustrates the important difference between providing a commander with raw intelligence giving him an interpretive best estimate based upon it.) The example also illustrates the relevance of and important principles of information management: a fact attested by several independent sources is strongly supported by this multiplicating even if those sources are individually weak.

When an aggregate estimate is based on an inference on reports of different levels of reliability, its evolution is generally based on the weakest link principle even as the chain is no stronger than its weakest link, so the countenance is not more secure than its least-reliable premise. But one critically important consideration is operative here, via the analog of a rope rather than a chain. For even as with ropes many frail strands can function cooperatively to create a strong tie, so with reports many *independent* but individually problematic reports can continue to achieve a high degree of reliability. When there is sufficient smoke, there is also liable to be a fire. When those reports arise independently of one another (and that is crucial), there is a marked increase in their reliability.

Another key aspect of report interpretation relates to the matter of what sort of response the report calls for on the recipient's part. Report access is not just a matter of asking, What does the report mean?, but also calls for asking, What does the report portend for the issues of our present agenda? This sort of problem is usually the more challenging and difficult. Relevancy to agenda issues is the crucial factor here, and interpretation is matter of examining the implications of a report for action in the wider range of presently germane concerns.

The interpretation of reports generally demands an extensive analysis of its relationship to the wider context of what is known or believed or conjectured. The salient questions are: How does what this report tells us amplify or modify what we already take ourselves to know; what are its implications for any advisable alterations in our plans for action; what if anything ought we to change in our projected agenda of action if what this report maintains is true? Interpretation accordingly has two major sectors in relation to possible revisions in thought (belief) and in action (behavior). It is a matter of eliciting the appropriate "implication" of the report for belief and action.

An observer's report that members of a certain military unit were observed at the front may mean to a regimental commander that the enemy has been reinforced, to the sector's commanding general that an offensive may shortly be launched against them, and to common soldiers that they will soon be contending with seasoned veterans rather than raw rookies.

The *plausibility* of a report hinges on the extent to which it harmonizes with preexisting information. Plausibility is one of the two paramount factors in determining the credibility of a report, with the other being the *reliability* of its sources.

A report that fits well into the setting of preestablished (or at any rate preaccepted) information will for this very reason deserve credence to an extent not necessarily reflected in the general reliability of its source. And of course the reverse situation will obtain as well. (This is a situation of which those who project deceit will seek to exploit by surrounding their disinformation with a larger context of plausible fact.)

The problem is that we invariably assess information against the background of a prevailing normativity and have a natural tendency to devalue (if not dismiss outright) those ideas that do not conform to preexisting patterns. Unless the anomalous and eccentric arrives in a way that is strikingly convincing, it is likely to be relegated to the outer periphery of attention and acknowledgment. It seems that a "normality tropism" of sorts is at work to induce us to reset two possibilities at zero.

One of the most insightful and instructive studies of intelligence reportage is Roberta Wohlstetter's 1962 analysis of intelligence information regarding Japan's planning of the Pearl Harbor attack.[16] Like every other study of the matter, its examination of the developments shows that the U.S. intelligence services and the larger authority to which they reported had ample and decisive evidence that Japan was about to launch extensive military operation in the western Pacific in response to American pressure via a variety of nemeses—especially an embargo on oil shipments to Japan. Just where the blow would fall was the only open question.

Now in this regard there were in fact many signs that Pearl Harbor was among the initial objectives, the fleet in its anchorage affording a prize target. The problem, however, was that there were many signs they were—in advance of the fact—no more than small eddies in the vast surrounding sea of information. They were, in effect, no more than whispers against the background of envisioning "noise."

Wohlstetter had the ingenious idea of resorting to technical conceptions from formal information theory as developed by Claude Shannon in the late 1940s. In particular, she invoked the idea of systemic noise to characterize the virtually random and meaningless clatter astir in the information at one's disposal. And this suggested use of the idea of *entropy* within a message system—negating the prospect of denying significant information about its operations.

By invoking these analogies and establishing their plausibility in the circumstances at issue with the information landscape of 1941 military and diplomatic intelligence, Wohlstetter found a natural and plausible explanation of the incapacity of the intelligence system of the day to pinpoint Pearl Harbor as where Japan's initial strike would fall.

Such an account has important implications. For it means that the responsibility for the surprise achieved by Japan at Pearl Harbor was not the result of incompetence or lack of dedication to duty of individual operatives but that it lay in the disfunctionality of an entire system, ill-suited to discern beliefs of systemic meaning within a massive background of discordant and seemingly incoherent information.

Even highly significant needles can get lost from sight in a haystack of others. In late 1941 American intelligence duty intercepted and decrypted requests from Tokyo to their agents in Honolulu for ongoing ungraded location reports of stamp anchorage in Pearl Harbor. But no one "connected the dots."

One of the important lessons to emerge from Wohlstetter's study is that the strongly hierarchical structure of monitoring and diplomatic organizations creates a gap between the technical expert, who coordinates and interprets intelligent information, and the higher level administrators and top commanders, who alone can determine actual implementation. Thus, in the case of Pearl Harbor, "only certain experts in the Far Eastern office of ONI [The Office of Naval Intelligence] and [the Army's intelligence branch] G2 had a proper view of the range and significance of this [communications intelligence] type of indicator, but their judgment unfortunately did not carry much weight outside their own divisions."[17] Interlinkage of communication and reciprocity of trust between producers, interpreters, and implementers of intelligence information is an indispensable desideratum in this domain.

At this point the theory of cognitive dissonance also becomes relevant.[18] When evidential indications come to view favoring a condition contrary to one's prevailing—which obviously favor the normal and accustomed—natural penchant for consistency and resistance of the discomfort of incoherence in belief so functions as to invite their dismissal.

A major issue in the management of reports is the problem of "mixed signals"—reports pointing toward different answers to the questions at issue, and the most difficult reports to interpret are those that do not conform to the indications of preestablished fact. In interpreting reports, conflicts and divergence must be ironed out and a coherent overall picture produced. Systematization and coordination must secure chains and settle the problem of mixed and dissonant signals, cognitive and the like in general. In the face of such dissonance, there is likely to be a strong—and often justified—inclination to dismiss the credibility of such reports.

And this means that coordination of effort and sharing of information among different units is of substantial value to intelligence services. In this regard the British made an immense contribution in the Second World War that put the Allies far ahead of their Axis adversaries—a circumstance that worked to their immense advantage.[19]

While a reporter can never guarantee the acceptance of a report, the reporter can take steps to increase the likelihood that its interpretation will issue in a favorable response. A reporter can ensure that its message is clear, its presentation plausible, its evidentiation made transparent, and its obstacles explained away. But in the final analysis, acceptance and implementation are matters that lie in other hands.

PRESUMPTION: GOING BEYOND THE TEXT

The cardinal rule of report interpretation is as follows: Take reports at face value and give a reported message the benefit of doubt insofar as your available evidence permits. A literal construal of reports is this is the default position that remains in place, until and unless some case-specific considerations come into view that cast doubt upon the matter. A report, just like an accused person in the U.S. legal system, is to be treated as innocent until proven guilty.

A major difficulty arises for report interpretation and stems from the misfortune of information insufficiency. For to make good interpretive sense of reports, we need to contextualize them in "the big picture" of relevant matters, and our realization of this desideratum is blocked in the face of informational insufficiency. How then to proceed?

Report interpretation involves conjectural projections, and we cannot invest much confidence in the matter until and unless confirmatory substantiation comes into view that enables us to transmute promising conjecture into plausible constructions. And one thing that is commonly done is to make presumptions.

Many reporting issues need never be addressed explicitly, but they stand subject to such standardly conventionalized suppositions as "Normalcy prevails in undiscussed matters." A sampling of such cognitive presumptions includes such principles as the following:

- The testimony of our senses is trustworthy.
- The information provided to us by reference works is correct.
- What people tell us is true.
- Reports will not deliberately depart from what their authors regard as the truth of things.
- In reporting, importantly relevant facts will not be omitted.

All of these generalizations will sometimes fail us: none is literally true as it stands. But this does not conflict with their status as presumptions. For in each case it is plausible—and reasonable—to proceed on this basis unless and until there are case-specific indications that this is not so in the situation at hand. It is, again, a standing presumption that the usual presumption of information processing provides us with adequate guidance.

Its reliance on a presumptive default to what is normal, typical, or the like, means that any interpretive process is inherently chancy. What is at issue with presumption is at bottom not an endorsement of a general truth but the implementation of a principle and, thus in effect, the adoption of a policy. And rationality here—as elsewhere in matters of practical procedure—pivots on the principle of a favorable balance of potential benefit over potential loss. In many situations default reasoning affords the best-available pathway to our ultimately very practical requirement for information—for answering in a cogent and circumstantially responsible way a question that we need to resolve. In a difficult world where we are often at a loss for needed information, the fruits of plausible reasoning will often have to serve us in place of seriously consolidated knowledge. The ruling idea is to fill in the blank spaces in a way that renders it only natural and plausible that the explored (known) region should be what it is.

And now of course the issue of testing comes to the fore. The task becomes one of striving to enlarge the range of relevant reporting—of enlarging the explored ground to see one's conjectures regarding the original terra incognita as able to be maintained, so as to confirm that those initial conjectures are able to stand secure and support new conjectures.

From the recipient's point of view, its fit within the overall framework of already accepted information is a central consideration for the acceptability of a report. The very fact that a certain item fits neatly into a system of what is taken as preestablished fact provides a powerful indication that "we've got it right" and affords us with a substantial item of evidence for it. The pursuit of consistency, consonance, coherence, completeness, and the like clearly characterize our pursuit of cognitive adequacy, seeing that the systematization of knowledge is a prime instrument of cognitive quality control.

There are in fact very different sorts of "errors." There are errors of the first kind—errors of omission arising when we do not accept the statement P when P is in fact the case. These involve the sanction (disvalue) of *ignorance*. And there are also errors of the second kind— errors of commission arising when we accept P when in fact not-P is the case. These involve the mark of cognitive dissonance and outright *mistake*. And clearly both sorts of missteps are *errors*. The rules of the cognitive game call not only for rejecting falsehoods and keeping the wrong things out but also for accepting truths and assuring that the right things get in. Systematization is a great help in these regards. It is presumptively error-minimizing with respect to the two kinds of cognitive errors. Given its coordinated stress on comprehensiveness and mutual fit, the systematization of our knowledge clearly facilitates the realization of its governing objective: the engrossing of information in the context of an optimal balance of truth over falsehood.

Given such a focus on probative and explanatory issues, the systematic interpretation of reports calls for three major interrelated functions:

1. *Intelligibility.* Systematicity is the prime vehicle for understanding; for it is just exactly their systematic interrelationships that render factual claims intelligible. As long as they remain discrete and disconnected, they lack any adequate handle for the intellect that seeks to take hold of them in its endeavor to comprehend the issues involved.

2. *Rational Organization.* Systematicity, in its concern for such desiderata as simplicity, uniformity, and so on, affords the means to a probatively rational and scientifically viable articulation and organization of our knowledge. The systematic development of knowledge is thus a key part of the idea of a science.

3. *Verification.* Systematicity is a vehicle of cognitive quality control. It is plausible to suppose that systematically developed information is more likely to be correct—or at any rate less likely to be defective—thanks to its avoidance of the internal error-indicative conflicts of discrepancy, inconsistency, and disuniformity. This indicates the service of systematization as a testing process for acceptability—an instrument of verification.

PREDISPOSITION AND MATTERS OF FACT

A report's fit into the prevailing atmosphere of belief makes all the difference. Some messages are "music to our ears"; we welcome them and make them beneficiaries of a pro-attitude. But then too other messages can be decidedly unwelcome and the subject of a con-attitude. Thus, we take some on board eagerly and secure them with open arms. Others we resist and charge with the impediment of added burdens of proof. Their going against preconceptions and—above all—going against affinities and predispositions are the prime causes of the misinterpretation of reports. When elements of the German army and security services reported to America's intelligence representatives in Switzerland late in the Second World War that there was considerable discontent among the senior military leadership with the Nazi system, dismay at the obviously unsuccessful war with its exposure of German cities to ever increasing bombardment, different members of the Allies had very different interpretations of these reports. The Americans took the reports at face value as indications of discontent and weariness in parts of the public and parts of the elite. Stalin, by contrast, viewed the American's willingness to receive those Germans messengers as an indication of an Anglo-American interest in making a separate peace with Germany at the Soviet Union's expense.[20] Strangely, both of Germany's most powerful enemies in the Second World War entertained totally unwarranted fears that the other might make a separate peace with Germany and interpreted their espionage reports in the light of that apprehension.[21]

Plausibility assessment is a matter of examining the extent to which a report fits with the context of the recipient's preexisting knowledge or putative knowledge. Reports that the Allied cross-channel invasion of France would come in Normandy were dismissed by the German high command because they had ample grounds—based not only on general principles but also on misleading evidence—for expecting an assault across the Pas-de-Calais. As anyone who has ever done textual proofreading knows well, we humans have a deeply ingrained tendency to see what we want to see—and not necessarily what we actually look at. Report reading is no exception to this rule.

In reaching its recipient a report enters a preexisting context—a "climate of opinion" or belief ethos—with which it must come to terms. And at this point there are three main possibilities.

- The ethos is *welcoming*: the report fits harmoniously into the fabric of prevailing belief.
- The ethos is *inimical*: there is cognitive dissonance and the report clashes with the tenor of prevailing belief.
- The ethos is *neutral*: the report neither supports nor counter-indicates what preexists but amplifies it in some way.

These relationships elicit distinctive reactions to the report on the recipient's part. With harmony there is a natural pro-inclination; there is a natural tendency to deem the report acceptable. With disharmony there is a natural con-inclination; there is a natural tendency to be skeptical about the report. With supplementation there is a natural tendency to give the report the benefit of doubt, deeming it as provisionally acceptable subject to further developments that might shed additional light on its claims.

In early 1941, Stalin was convinced on general principles that Hitler did not want a two-front war. On the basis of this prejudgment he dismissed Churchill's warning of the impending attack in June as a British trick to embroil him with Germany. And similarly, he scoffed at Russian master spy Richard Sorge's similar report from Tokyo as further disinformation. Distrust of Britain ran too deep in Stalin's views to permit any other conclusion. However, later on when Sorge reported in September 1941 that Japan was unwilling to attack Soviet forces in Manchuria, Stalin accepted this and transferred some fifteen divisions from Siberia to Europe in time for their much needed use in the defense of Moscow. Whatever can be interpreted can be misinterpreted, and even the best of reports is useless when it comes to an ear unwilling to listen.

In the wake of Germany's invasion of Russia, there came to light the mass-murder of thousands of Polish army officers by the retreating

Russian forces in the Katyn forest in the Russian zone of Poland. The subsequent Red Cross report of the barbarism of their ally came as decidedly unwelcome news to the Western Allies, whose officials, while knowing better, encouraged the media to regard this as mere Nazi propaganda. In the United States during the war this horrific episode was accordingly given restricted distribution and little credence.

PROBLEMS FOR INTERPRETERS

The appropriate exploitation of expert knowledge is crucial in intelligence interpretation. And here the so-called Delphi method has substantial promise. Originally conceived for specifically predictive applications (especially in matters of technological forecasting), it can render good service in working toward a consensus among conflicting expert estimates.[22]

In matters of interpretation, intelligence operations are bound to exhibit an unwelcome tension. Ideally, they would like to have a narrower range of access on a tightly restricted "need to know" basis to protect against penetration. But the need for interpretation via contextualization means that broad access must be provided if interpreters are to do their job well. The partitioning that security demands is counterproductive for effective interpretation, which requires access to "the big picture." And the traditional solution—that is, to provide such access only to those at the top of the organizational chart—runs into the difficulty that there are bound to be people of wide-ranging responsibility who simply don't have the time to dedicate due care to interpretational complexities.

Yet another tension arises in relation to confidential reports in national security matters—be they military or diplomatic. For if such reports are to be properly understood and exploited, they must be properly interpreted—an achievement that requires wide knowledge of relevant issues on the part of report users. And yet secrecy and security calls for a divided access to information on a strictly construed "need to know" basis. There arises a conflict between understanding and confidentially that is pervasive in intelligence operations.

In matters of military or diplomatic intelligence, the most fundamental problems in integrating reports are the ever-present irony of "plants" and the turning of information into disinformation. The entire reportage scene sometimes turns into a "hall of mirrors," where nothing is what it looks to be and nothing means what it says. The differences can be perceived only on the basis of a deep knowledge of the entire body of available information—if then.

For reasons of security, intelligence agencies do well to compartmentalize information. Inevitably, however, this is at odds with the interpretation and, above all, utilization of a report. It is at this juncture that the operation becomes more vulnerable to penalties, sabotage, and betrayal. Security and implementation are functions that invariably conflict in this domain.

CHAPTER 8

EVALUATION

REPORT MERITS

The evaluation of reports involves many different factors and puts a wide variety of issues upon the agenda:

- Regarding acceptability/correctness
  - —probable vs. improbable
  - —well evidentiated vs. ill evidentiated
  - —accurate vs. inaccurate
- Regarding significance
  - —informative vs. uninformative
  - —important vs. unimportant
  - —novel vs. redundant
  - —norm-conforming vs. eccentric
- Regarding formulation
  - —detailed vs. vague
  - —clear vs. unclear
  - —definite vs. ambiguous
  - —convoluted vs. straightforward

The inherent value of a report can be measured in quasi-economic terms, with its value to the reporter being measured by the extent of resources he or she is willing to expend in order to provide it, and its value to the receiver measured by the extent of the resources he or she is prepared to expend to obtain it. But these are purely notional conceptions. For with useful information, as with the air we breathe, we do not generally have to pay a price commensurate with its worth.

Overall, reports can exhibit a considerable variety of merits as per the tabulation of table 3. But where there is merit, there is demerit as well, and in reporting there are many possible missteps. Many of these arise with the reporting process and from the prospect that:

- the original information is incorrect misinformation
- the reporting agent misunderstands or misrepresents the transmitted information
- the transmission process mangles or distorts the transmitted information
- the reported information is viewed as flawed

Reportage is a machine of many moving parts, all of which can malfunction. No component part of the process is failproof: the whole enterprise is a minefield of potential error.

Reporting accordingly cries out for the evaluative assessment and grading of its products. And here the first and most crucial factor is that of a report's credibility to its intended recipients. For however true and accurate an actionable report may be, it is useless if its recipient does not accept it at the time (and thus often in advance of the fact). The recipient has to be convinced that the report has a solid basis of substantiation and is not a matter of sheer guesswork and idle conjecture.

The management of intelligence reports in times of international crisis can suffer from data swamping, since an organization designed to function in normal circumstances can readily become flooded and overstretched in such circumstances. It then becomes difficult to process the mass of available information even to the point of an inability

TABLE 3. REPORTORIAL MERITS

RELIABILITY INTENSIVE

Virtues of Informants/Information-Bases/Sources
(The originating sources of information)
- relevant knowledge/possession of information
- candor/willingness to provide information

Virtues of Reporters/Information Agents/Information Gatherers
(Those who gain access to and report information)
- access to information and informants
- conscientiousness/commitment/dedication
- trustworthiness/reliability
- security mindedness (where needed)

Virtues of Transmitters/Information Forwarders
(Those who transmit information to its recipients)
- effective transmission management
- trustworthiness/reliability
- secure transmission management

PLAUSIBILITY INTENSIVE

Virtues of Reportees/Report-Recipients
(Those who receive report information)
- attentiveness/effective information management
- honesty in informing
- knowledgeable utilization/implementation of information

Virtues of the Reports Themselves
(The information that is transmitted to the recipients)
- correctness and accuracy
- fit/plausibility
- balance between paucity and prolixity (i.e. sufficiency of information)
- care for security and source confidentiality where needed.

UTILITY INTENSIVE

Virtues of the Reports Significance
- informative importance

Virtues of Report Implementability
- relevance to reportee needs and goals
- convenience of information access (ease of process)
- timeliness

to separate the important from the background of the insignificant. Providing useful information to consumers in a timely basis can then become effectively impossible.[1]

While often there is a situation of insufficient information, sometimes the reverse is the case, there occasionally being an information glut with so many reports arriving that it becomes difficult to tell the sheep from the goats. Only statistical scanning or large-scale survey can single out what is worthwhile. In such matters there are few general rules of procedure because appropriate procedures must be too closely attuned to the specifics of the situation.

And there is yet another form of information glut—one whose perplexity lies not just in quantitative excess but in qualitative incoherence in that the problem becomes one of inconsistency. Some of the reports conflict with others; some point up and others down; information becomes jumbled up with misinformation. Here again, statistical indications apart, general rules are of little use and case specific expertise is required for effective proceedings.

ACCEPTANCE ISSUES

Apart from simply ignoring it altogether, there are three ways to respond to the arrival of a report: *to accept*, *to reject* (by seeing it as false and thus accepting its negation), or *to suspend* judgment. Of these three reactions, both of the first two yield information; the third leaves the issue undecided. Rejecting a report is clearly called for when one already has information that indicates its falsity. It may, however, also be in order—and then actually provides new information—when one has good reasons to believe that the reporter is engaged in deception, thereby serving as a reliable indicator of falsehood.

The acceptance of reports hinges on their credibility, and a report is *credible* to the extent that there is good reason for its acceptance. Three factors are paramount determinants of credibility:

- *plausibility of substance*: the extent to which the report harmonizes with information otherwise at hand
- *reliability of reporters*: the track record of reporters on cognitive issues in the past
- *consilience of sources*: the extent to which independently functioning sources provide similar indications

Consilient reports that are independently arrived at are worth their weight in gold. For even though any one of them taken by itself may be questionable and inconclusive, it is unlikely that all of them are wrong. And of course even if only one of them is right regarding the issue, that settles the matter.[2] For here context matters. Even an otherwise doubtful report can achieve credibility if also substantiated by further confirmations. (Many weak threads can make up a strong rope.)

In evaluating reports the critical appraisal range is not correct-incorrect or true-false, since this is generally not determinable *at the time*. Rather it will have to be something like credible-dubious or trustworthy-doubtful.

Incorrect, let alone deliberately deceitful, reports do not arrive wearing little red flags. The sheep and the goats do not come into view as such—they are effectively indistinguishable. Separating the good from the bad is often possible only with the wisdom of hindsight.

Of course, one way to enhance the credibility of a report is to diminish its specificity and detail. It is safer to claim that some troops are being moved into a sector than to affirm that it is exactly one regiment, and less liable to error to claims this than to say it is the 103rd Panzer. So a reporter must be careful with detail: on the one hand, providing detail enhances credibility by its aura of being well informed; on the other hand, it injects an element of vulnerability.

The confidence level that interpreters credit reports resembles the "degrees of knowledge" familiar in philosophical epistemology. The situation at issue here is sketched out in the tabulation of table 4. One could of course quantify these classifications on a confidence scale of 1 to 10 or to 100. But it then needs to be borne in mind that such confidence values do not behave like probabilities. For example, if the probability of a claim p is low then that of not-p will have to be high. But if one source reports something (p) that is rather implausible, so that our confidence in this claim (p) is low, while another generally credible source contradicts this (i.e., affirms not-p), then we might well meet this claim with skepticism.

A two-factor scheme for assessing overall report acceptability was employed in British intelligence in the Second World War. The workings of this scheme has been described as follows in a biography of its originator, Admiral J. H. Godfrey, then Britain's director of naval intelligence:

> Reports received in the Naval Intelligence Directorate (NID) from [MI5's chief] 'C', the Foreign Office, or indeed any other source, rarely contained any very precise or clear indication of their authenticity or probability. 'From a usually reliable source', 'From an unknown source' and similar expressions were helpful in their way but such qualifications were not always included and were in any case too long-winded and imprecise for incorporation in signals to ships and Flag Officers at sea. [NID's chief] Admiral J. H. Godfrey wanted something short and concise which would immediately convey to the recipient the exact degree of trust which should be placed in any particular piece of information.

TABLE 4. LEVELS OF INFORMATIVE CONFIDENCE

Probative Classification	Strength of Substantiation	Confidence Level
Suspicions and surmises	very weak	very low
Plausible conjectures	weak	low
Reasonable beliefs	moderate	middling
Demonstrations	strong	high
Proofs	conclusive	very high

Like all great ideas it was so simple that one cannot understand why it had not been thought of before.

Each item of intelligence received in NID was assessed and graded for reliability from A to E for source and 1 to 5 for contents. Thus A1 would indicate that a report had come from a completely reliable source and that the information it contained was regarded by NID as factual. B4 would show that though the source was good the information itself was thought to be unlikely, while a D2 assessment meant that despite the poor or virtually unknown nature of the source the report itself seemed highly probable. Furthermore, any deductions drawn from the information contained in the text had to be separated from the facts by the word 'Comment'. An additional virtue of the system was that it compelled intelligence officers to consider all information they received with great care and to accept a degree of personal responsibility when giving it further circulation.[3]

On this basis, Admiral Godfrey's report grading scheme took the form summarized in table 5.

TABLE 5. ADMIRAL GODFREY'S GRADING SCHEME FOR ASSESSING REPORT ACCEPTABILITY/CREDIBILITY

	SOURCE RELIABILITY	CONTENT PLAUSIBILITY
VERY HIGH	A	1
HIGH	B	2
MIDDLING	C	3
LOW	D	4
VERY LOW	E	5

Note: The result of applying this "Godfrey Scale" of report assessment would then be a twenty-five compartment classification ranging from A1 to E5.

However, for actual use Admiral Godfrey's approach was perhaps a bit too sophisticated. Complexity may help to ease the conscience of the transmitter of a report but for the recipient's point of view there is a simpler issue: Is the reported ramification reliable or not? And so for reasons of ease of complementation, one might well simplify Admiral Godfrey's evaluation scheme into the more compact, tripartite classification of: high (H), middling (M), and low (L). This would suffice for most practical purposes, if only because more fine-grained distinctions are not all that easily understood and implemented in the usual course of things, seeing that anyhow in most cases the trustworthiness of the sources and the plausibility of the reports are factors one cannot estimate with great exacting precision. Such a reduced grounding process will result in a grading scheme for reports based on a more compact nine-compartment scale (3 × 3) ranging from HH to LL. This proceeding yields the combined results of the following nine-category tabulation:

	H	M	L
H	HH	HM	HL
M	MH	MM	ML
L	LH	LM	LL

Reliability (label to the left of the M row)

This grading procedure in turn invites a still simpler, one-dimensional comparison five-category scheme on a single "school grade" ranging from A to F as per:

Plausibility

A	B	C
B	C	D
C	D	F

Reliability (label to the left of the B C D row)

On this basis a single letter would convey a reasonable first approximation schema for accessing the overall acceptability and value of a report, as per:

Very High: A (secure)
High: B (highly reliable)
Middling: C (reliable)
Low: D (credible)
Very Low: F (conjectural)

Such a simplified overall grading procedure accommodates both of the parameters at issue in Admiral Godfrey's two-dimensional report-assessment scheme, with both reliability and plausibility factored in. In the absence of case-specific indications to the contrary, it provides a usable rule of thumb for assessing cognitive outcomes on the basis of the subsidiary merits of course reliability and report plausibility.

When a report's credibility is in some doubt, one would in practice obviously want to set the acceptance threshold in line with the magnitude of the stake at risk. And moreover one would in any event prefer to postpone a decision while awaiting further developments—at least in those matters where delay occasions no further penalties or risks.

All the same, when there is a question for which an answer is imperatively needed then we simply have to do the best we can. In such circumstances the answers that best fit in with the envisioned body of relevant information will have to be accepted—at least provisionally. Here as elsewhere one has to rest satisfied with the best that can be done in the circumstances—like it or not.

SOURCE RELIABILITY AND CONTENT PLAUSIBILITY

An instructive insight emerges when one arithmetizes those salient factors of reliability and plausibility. For if we allot 1, 2, 3 to high, middling, and low, respectively, it emerges from this quantified perspective that the comparative accessibility ranking of a report can in general be represented as a product of the source reliability and content plausibility, as per the equation Report Credibility = (Source Reliability) × (Content Plausibility), and then combine the result multiplicatively via the quantity *Reliability × Plausibility*, and we will then obtain a single composite numerical assessment of overall acceptability. And the nine entries of that initial 3 × 3 scheme will now receive the following scores:

Plausibility

	1	2	3
Reliability	2	4	6
	3	6	9

Given this mode of arithmetization, we can now reconceptualize the preceeding five-fold classifications of overall report acceptability:

1: secure (A)
2: highly reliable (B)
3–4: reliable (C)
5–6: credible (D)
7 + : conjectural (F)

On this basis, we recover exactly the same five-category array already encountered above.[4] This, of course, is less informative than the more elaborate British scheme but may well prove sufficient for most practical purposes. However, this multiplicative approach could also be applied on an extended basis to arithmetize more elaborate grading schemes such as Admiral Godfrey's five-fold evaluation scheme, which would then yield an evaluative scheme ranging from A to 25.[5]

OVERALL SIGNIFICANCE

The credibility of a report involves issues entirely different from its significance. These two factors are quite independent. A seemingly significant report may lack credibility, and a highly credible one may lack significance. It is only when there is a coordination here, when a report is both credible and significant; that is, actually of substantial importance.

Once the credibility of a report has been favorably assessed, the question of its significance will immediately arise. This itself has two aspects; namely, *practical significance* (the extent to which it deflects our *course of action* in providing motivating impetus to acting differently than we otherwise would) and *cognitive significance* (the extent to which it deflects our system of belief in providing grounds for believing differently than we otherwise would).

Cognitive significance is a matter of a report's informativeness. Practical significance, by contrast, hinges on its utility, the extent to which it is *actionable*—operationally useful so that something can and should be done about it.

Both cognitive and practical importance now enter upon the scene as critical factors in assessing a report's overall significance. For reports serve both to enhance knowledge and to guide action. Here actionability is a matter of the *extent* to which the recipient can and should act on the information of the report (ranging from "highly actionable" to "nothing to be done about it"). And *urgency* is a matter of time pressure—of the indication action, ranging from "urgent and immediate" to eventually, "whenever time permits."

Both actionability and urgency can in principle be graded as per the tripartite grading scheme high, middling, and low that we have already put to work elsewhere. (Winston Churchill's notorious "Action this day" would reflect reportage at the high-high level of top priority reactivity.)[6]

In the end, then, assessing the overall significance of reports calls for resolving a cascade of questions that arise in the natural course of things.

Is the report credible?
If so, is it informative?

If so, is it actionable?
If so, is it urgent?

In the end it is important to realize that with respect to reports acceptability and probability are two different and substantially independent issues. In some circumstances of reportage an inherently improbable claim may deserve acceptance and, contrariwise, a very probable one may need to be rejected. The probative situation in matters of reportage presents a complex challenge, the sensible resolution of which requires close attention to matters of epistemological detail attuned to the specific purposes of the evaluative enterprise at issue.

PRIORITY IN PROCESSING REPORTS

In reaching to reports, timing is not only a factor in implementation but also in processing. For when an extensive body of reports require analysis and interpretation, a preliminary evaluation becomes necessary to guide the overall process. And here a recipient has a choice between two alternatives. The one procedure is to begin with those reports that rank highly in terms of their utility and then to seek out the most informative among these. And the other procedure is effectively to reverse this procedure, beginning with the most informative reports and then to seek out the most urgently actionable.

Again, there are no hard-and-fast rules here. Proper processing prioritization depends on the prevailing conditions. In particular, the question of what starting-point category is of a smaller and thereby more manageable size. But in any case, preliminary evaluation is a crucial first step in reducing the mass-management of reportage to practically manageable proportions.

APPENDIX

As already noted, the major dimensions of report value are credibility, informativeness, and actionability. And so once the issue of a report's acceptance is settled, two priority issues remain: its informative significance and its actionability. Each of these three factors can be assessed on the 1–3 scale of high, middling, and low. When this is done, we obtain a twenty-seven-compartment scheme of report evaluation ranging from $1 \times 1 \times 1 = 1$ to $3 \times 3 \times 3 = 27$. And we would again resort to the idea of a multiplicatively combined reduction of this scheme into a series of letter grades as per

    A: 1–4
    B: 5–6
    C: 8–9
    D: 9–12
    F: > 12

As this illustration indicates, a relatively compact grading scheme can in theory (and presumably in practice) be used to convey a plausible indication of the overall merit of reports in a way that takes some account of the complexity of the issue in its diversified complexity.

To be sure, this particular approach treats all three of the major parameters of report as alike and thus as equally significant. Whenever a more refined grading is needed, appropriate modifications will be required.[7]

In any event, the evaluation of reports is altogether essential, and for various practical purposes, it is useful to providing the outcome in a simplified summary form. However, when this is done it must never be forgotten that in actual fact a plurality of fundamentally different sorts of considerations have to come into play.

It is clear that the proper management of reports is a complex process. Before being put to useful work they must be considered, interpreted, and evaluated. By and large people do this informally on their own. But on a larger scale in enterprises that depend on large-scale report exploration, such as diplomatic or intelligence centers, this sort of thing becomes a highly technical and specialized activity whose proper exercise requires people who are well informed, experienced, and endowed with good judgment. In these contexts report exploitation is a difficult and demanding business whose effective management in actual practice is—for understandable reasons—rather the exception than the rule.

Interesting theoretical questions arise regarding mechanics of inference in these contexts. Let it be that one seeks the judgment of several (independent) sources as to the truth of some factual claim. Let it further be that the sources are graded in terms of reliability (high, middling, and low). And let f the truth-likelihood of the claim at issue also be graded in this range (high, middling, and low) by the various sources. We can now proceed as follows: For the i-th source we assign a "source-weight" (W) of 4, 2, or 1 according as the source reliability is H, M, or L, respectively. And we further assign a source likelihood quotient (Q_i) of 3, 2, or 1 accordingly as that source judges the likelihood of the claim at issue as H, M, or L, respectively. And we then assign to that contention an "aggregate acceptability index" consisting of the average of the contentions of those varying sources:

$$\mu = \frac{1}{n} \Sigma \ W_i \times Q_i$$

This approach accommodates the intuition that (1) we acknowledge acceptability on the basis of the individual appraisals of our sources, and (2) that in effecting this judgment we acknowledge that a sufficient number of independent low-reliability sources can outweigh the judgment of those of higher reliability.

Machinery of this sort can be instructively helpful in dealing with larger issues. It can, for example, instructively address the issue of belief revision in the light of additional information.[8] The problem here has the following structure: Let it be that n varied "sources" (be they persons or theories) give a ruling on some factual contention (either in the range true-false or in that of high, middling, or low probability). And now let it be that a new "source" comes along and provides an additional judgment in the matter. How is this to affect our aggregate appraisal of the acceptability of this contention? The indicated machinery can clearly provide an effective mechanism for dealing with problems of this sort.

CHAPTER 9
UTILIZATION

THE PRAGMATIC ASPECT OF REPORTAGE

Information that remains inert and unused is effectively pointless. The prime function of useful reportage is to yield information for the effective guidance of action. Recipients accordingly tend to take a utilitarian view of reports as serving either their cognitive or their practical interests. As Admiral C. M. Forbes of Britain's Royal Navy complained to Admiral J. H. Godfrey in the Directory of Naval Intelligence in 1942 with regard to over-restrictive security regulations "however secret may be the source . . . intelligence can never be an end in itself, and if it does not lead to action, it is valueless."[1]

Britain's creation of elaborate administrative mechanisms in the Second World War to ensure that the information provided by its intelligence agencies was swiftly transmitted to and actually used by those who managed operations "in the field" was a revolutionary accomplishment and made an important contribution to war management.

Perhaps the best-ever remunerated report was John Stuart Mill's 1858 report on the East India Company's stewardship of the subcontinent. Intended to salvage the company's reputation after the nationalization of its holdings in the wake of the Sepoy Mutiny, this report's powerful defense of the company's stewardship of Indian affairs was so effective that the appreciative directors rewarded Mill with the handsome sum of £5,000. They got their money's worth with a report that Lord Grey, the colonial secretary, described as the best state paper he had ever seen.[2]

Many reports merely evoke the acknowledgment of "Hmm, interesting" in the recipient. But not all will do so. Some energize their recipients into action. Specifically, actionable reports are those whose basis the recipient does or should indicate an action of some kind—reports that cry out for a responsive effort. From a receiver's point of view the single most significant feature beyond the truth of a report is its actionability through the prospect of using the information it provides in guiding potentially beneficial action. This fact renders timely warning reports regarding tsunamis or bomb threats of paramount value. Unfortunately, it also opens them up to misuse or abuse. False bomb threats are bound to have a destabilizing effect on the lives of their recipients and also pose the added danger of an eventual nonresponse in the face of the "crying wolf" phenomenon.

Both legally (job searches) and illegally (insider-information exploitation) obtained information is useful for guiding people's actions. Reports are valued for their utility: the most valued reports are those whose information provides incentive and guidance to actions. Reports that facilitate our efforts to achieved goals or to avert harms deserve to be—and are—generally prized. And at that point there is no limit. The range of possible report uses has a vastness beyond viable classification.

Especially in situations of substantial complexity, having information is one thing and being able to put it to effective use another. In conflict situations it is those who manage reporting of enemy activity who are best informed about what is going on on "the opposite side." This sometimes makes for awkward relations with the decision makers of their own side who have their own views and predilections—and illusions. In the summer of 1945, it was Japan's foreign office with its extensive access to political and military information via neutral nations that saw most clearly that the war was effectively lost. Convincing the other power brokers at the top level of government had to await the arrival of atomic bombs.

In matters of military or diplomatic intelligence, report reception is only the beginning of a long process leading to action. Even after a report is accessed, there is still the matter of its interpretation—of determining what it means within the context of otherwise available information. Only then, when a report's implications are amply understood, comes the crucial matter of implementation—of utilizing the reported information for the furtherance of one's objectives. And in reporting implementable information, the provider would generally do well to adjoin his best estimate of its actionable significance.[3]

The crucial job of any intelligence operative is to determine not just what should be reported but also who are to be the recipients of such a report. Issues of "need to know," potential implementation, and security maintenance are all crucial ingredients in such a complicated pot of brew.

With targeted and untargeted reports alike, the reporter will normally expect that the intended recipients make a suitable response to a report. Insofar as a reporter can prejudge the matter, he or she will—or at any rate should—design their report with a view to realizing this objective, keeping in mind the matter of what is to be of use to the recipients.

Often reports are replies to recipient requests, destined to provide something responsive to special needs. And even as people themselves are generally in the best position to make judgments about their goals, so they generally are in the best position to evaluate the utility of reports. Other people apart from the recipients may well be in a better position to evaluate the *truthfulness* of a report, but the intended recipient is generally best situated to access its *usefulness* in the setting of aims and objectives. Utility in terms of interest relevancy and implementational actionability is the paramount value of reports.

Instructive light is cast upon the agenda that report recipients customarily have by looking at the topical organization of the content of newspapers. Newspapers standardly divide their reportage into different sections as per:

- news
- finance
- culture and entertainment
- sports
- comics and amusement

This physical arrangement of reportage presumably mirrors the pattern of general readership concerns, with serious matters of politics (news) and investment (finance) first, eventually yielding to leisure interests (sports) and entertainment (comics)—though one suspects that for many readers the ordinary is actually reversed.

Among the most useful information espionage services can supply is reportage about what our enemy's espionage services are up to. At times there is even collusion between two such services with each putting the other into a position to earn brownie points with the control center back home—a field replete with insights into what the opposition does and does not know.

With reporting in general—but especially with matters of military intelligence—it transpires that even the best, most extensive, and accurate reporting is effectively useless in the absence of due provision for its use—its proper interpretation, exploitation, and implementation. From the very outset of the Second World War, the British intelligence services organized a complex procedure for the secure and effective transmission of information to field commanders who were in a position to make use of it. The Americans had nothing analogous in place, but they soon replicated British practice and were greatly benefited by this borrowing.

RISK

In accepting and implementing reports, we invariably run a risk of error, be it of omission and incompleteness or of commission and error. In fact these two modes of error trade off against one another. For when our acceptance standards are high, the one (omission) comes to the fore, and when they are too low, the other arises.

In general there are two fundamentally different kinds of misfortunes possible in situations of cognitive risk:

1. We reject something that, as it turns out, we should have accepted. We decline to take the chance, avoid running the risk at issue; things turn out favorably after all, but we lose out on the gamble.
2. We accept something that, as it turns out, we should have rejected. We take the chance and run the risk at issue, but things go wrong and we lose the gamble.

Clearly, the reasonable thing to do is to adopt a policy that minimizes misfortunes overall. It is thus evident that both type 1 and type 2 approaches will, in general, fail to be rationally optimal. Both approaches engender too many misfortunes for comfort. The sensible and prudent thing is to adopt the middle-of-the-road policy of risk calculation, striving as best we can to balance the positive risks of outright loss against the negative ones of lost opportunity. Rationality thus counterindicates approaches of type 1 and type 2, taking the line of the counsel. Neither avoid nor court risks but manage them prudently in the search for an overall minimization of misfortunes. The rule of reason calls for sensible management and a prudent calculation of risks; it standardly enjoins upon us the Aristotelian golden mean between the extremes of risk avoidance and risk seeking.

We generally grant reports the benefit of doubt. Barring contextual indications to the contrary, we view them as credible and confirmatively relevant. But such concessions are no more than provisional. They involve presumptions made for the sake of economy of effort. Yet by and large we recipients are fair weather friends to reports, prepared to abandon them in the wake of couterindications. Essentially, when acceptance involves risks, we naturally incline to the idea of playing safe. Ultimately, we face a question of value trade-offs. Are we prepared to run a greater risk of mistakes to secure the potential benefit of an enlarged understanding? In the end, the matter is one of priorities and values—safety against information, an epistemological risk-aversion against the impetus to understanding—where one must weigh the negativity of unknowing and incomprehension against the risk of mistakes and misinformation.

REACTIONS TO REPORTS: MATTERS OF IMPLEMENTATION

The potential of a report being used as a guide to action is accordingly one of its key features. From the recipient's point of view, a pivotal issue is going to be that of "What am I to do about it?" In the end, the value of a report lies in utilitarian considerations—in its capacity to serve the needs and wants of its intended recipients. (Secondarily, it may of course also have value for others.)

Reports of problematic situations are often as not requests for or injunctions to action. An SOS does not merely report imminent danger but enjoins "come help us!" The tenant's report to his landlord of a water leak is not just informative. Many sorts of reports invite or even demand appropriate action on the part of their intended recipients and are not given "for information only".[4] In fact, the action that is called for in response to a report is often so obvious and natural that the line between reporting and instructing—between reports and injunctions to action—become blurred (again, an SOS that an endangered ship at sea sends out to others is a good example here).

When one country's spies report that some other nation has managed to infiltrate an agent into its diplomatic mission there, they are more than likely to take appropriate countermeasures. Of course, there is a considerable spectrum of possibilities: we can simply expel the individual, proceed to feed them misinformation, or conceivably even arrange an accident that removes them from the scene. The choice of alternatives—the manifold of responses that characterize our use of the information—is a set of alternative possibilities that are motivated but nowise determined by the report itself. A report occasions choices but does not prescribe the outcomes.

It is one thing to have access to actionable reports and another to make use of them—even when the report receivers themselves are the relevant decision makers. Despite detailed reportage on Japan's just-accomplished attack on Pearl Harbor and certain knowledge of the movement of Japanese's forces toward his command in the Philippines, General Douglas MacArthur's war planes were caught on the ground when the attack came.[5]

However, even a highly actionable report is sometimes given with the explicit understanding that it *not* be acted upon. This occasion occurs in matters of insider trading, where the reported information should not be used for personal profit. And it also occurs in contexts of national security, where acting on a report may compromise its source to the determinant of greater potential benefits in the future.

Often the report recipients and its implementers are distinct from one another. Here once again special problems of transmission will arise and special arrangements must be made to connect those who have information and those who make operational use of it. In military contexts in particular, there is an inescapable need for organizational arrangement to connect reportage with operational planning, and large problems arise when this linkage does not function smoothly.

The most useful reports are those whose acceptance puts their recipients into a position to embark on a potentially productive course of action they could not otherwise undertake. Advance knowledge of the enemy's machinations is useless when no forces are available for countermeasures. (This, in effect, was the predicament of the British when Germany invaded Cyprus in the Second World War.) But even when such forces are amply available, this strength must actually be put into motion and effectively utilized. The information developed by intelligence must be transmitted to the field and actually used for the guidance of appropriate command decisions. This requires the creation and activation of an intelligence implementable shift, intermediating between the producers of intelligence at home and the commanders in the field.

To be sure, the prospect of an effective utilization of reports requires the recipient to preside over the assets and resources required for successful implementation. Even the most timely and accurate report of the enemy's plans, intensions, and actions is of no use to the commander whose forces are insufficient to take appropriate countermeasures.

NON-UTILIZATION AND SECRECY MANAGEMENT

As doctors, financiers, and secret agents well know, it is sometimes essential to restrict information access for reasons of personal privacy, commercial practice, national security, or the like. Such confidentiality requires some process of information access to be conducted under conditions of secrecy.

After all, you—or your representative—can gain access to the funds that a financial institution holds in your name by reporting to this organization a mass of information about yourself. And of course, if this information is intercepted by some third party, you lose control of your assets. In this context the claim that "information is money" is literally true. Secrecy of information—*confidentiality* as it is euphemistically called—is of the essence here. And the same is even more emphatically the case where the safeguarding of state secrets is concerned.

Throughout the realm of secrecy protection—alike in its human and its mechanical dimension—there is a systemic unwillingness among its managerial elite to admit the vulnerability of the enterprise and acknowledge the prospect that one's reportage is not secure.[6] (Granted, throughout the Second world War the top-level codes of the United States, the United Kingdom, and the Soviet Union remained secure from penetration. But the rise of the electronic computer has changed the situation.)

Monitoring secrecy is a Janus-faced requirement that must look in two directions. Internally, it must worry about betrayal—or at least a carelessness that is almost as bad. Externally, it must worry about penetration and "hacking." Often having no report at all is far preferable to having one that also reaches its unintended recipients.

In innumerable situations—matters of national security, commercial secrecy, police operations, and the like—the limitation of access to information is of prime importance. Protecting the security of its reports against unauthorized access is essential to the functioning of the enterprise. In such situations it is appropriate, inherent, and necessary to limit access to those who have a "need to know." In his "basic order" of January 11, 1940, Hitler mandated that "No one, no functionary, no officer, may learn about an official secret if this individual does not absolutely need to know about it,"[7] and his opponents did much the same.

Secrets are not created equal: some are more sensitively confidential than others and accordingly "deeper." In national security matters they are accordingly classified confidential, secret, and top secret.

How secret a secret is depends on the extent of change that could be caused through accession by unauthorized recipients. But who decides? Generally, it is the intended recipient for whose purposes the secret information is being supplied.[8] In matters of secrecy there is an agreement—a contract, as it were, be it legal or moral—between sender and receiver that their transaction is subject to confidentiality. On this basis, a breach of secrecy by either sender or receiver is an act of betrayal. Secrecy, after all, is a matter of trust: people are *entrusted* with secrets. But of course in this regard trust is not something that should be given freely; it has to be earned. With state secrets the greatest designed prevails at the top of the ladder. (Wilhelm Canaris and Kim Philby illustrate this point—albeit in very different ways and degrees.)

Moreover, this "need to know" principle regarding access to state secrets itself poses substantial difficulties. For when information is divided and different pieces of the puzzle are available only to different interpreters, no single operative will be able to "connect the dots." And so, paradoxical tension arises at this point with interpretation and secrecy as compelling factors. For making overt operational use of intelligence information is to acknowledge its possession and thereby compromises its secrecy. And sometimes a large price is required for maintaining secrecy. Thus despite advance warning about the massive raid in Coventry provided by signal intelligence, Churchill mandated an absence of protective measures lest Bletchley Park's penetration of German communications become unmasked.[9]

Moreover, another sort of tension arises in this connection—a conflict of personalities. The *interpretation* of reports requires technical expertise, the possession of wide and deep knowledge characteristic of theorists and and professorial types. But the *implementation* of reports requires decision makers, commanders, decisively active movers and shakers. Persons of these two types are not naturally drawn to feel personal or professional congeniality, and the trust and cooperativeness among individuals of these two types required for effective report management is not easily developed.

And yet another complication arises. Maintaining secrecy calls for division of access and the separating of information into disjoint silos. But this impedes the panoramic access needed for proper interpretation and affective implementation. The utility of intelligence information is secretly compromised when "the right hand does not know what that the left hand is doing." German experience throughout the Second World War as well as American experience in the prewar era, both vividly illustrate the price paid for fragmented intelligence operations by compartmentalization among different and often competing branches of service and agencies.[10]

There are two different ways in which someone can become the unintended recipient of a report:

1. by actively seeking out and obtaining information they are not intended to have—that is, by *prying* or even *spying*—or
2. by passively being given information they are not intended to have—that is, through *leakage* or even *betrayal*.

Whenever confidentiality of reporting matters, due care must be taken to guard against active and passive reportage compromise.

In the background of the topic of reportage lies the issue of a "right to information." This of course goes above and beyond the present topic of report epistemology. Suffice it here to say that ordinarily, its intended recipients are the only people entitled to access to a report. (Of course access to the *information* of a report is another issue.) The extent to which a report is deemed secret is inversely proportional to the size of the group of its intended recipients.

There is also the cognate issue of an obligation to report. We expect U.S. presidents to release their income tax returns and perhaps also their annual physical checkups. But the obligation at issue belongs to the presidents, not to the IRS or to their personal physicians.

The proverbial saying has it that "Actions speak louder than words," and along these lines there are various situations in which something is overtly done vis-à-vis opponents in order "to send them a message." Thus, in the summer of 1945, Japan asked Soviet Russia to mediate a cessation of hostilities with the Allied powers. Stalin's response was to unleash the Soviet Union's Siberian Red Army divisions on Japan's forces in Manchuria. This sort of "reporting" certainty conveyed the idea that was on his mind.

Secrecy can be fostered many different ways, with information protected by various distinctive devices. Prominent among these are

- *misinformation*: the provision of false and fact-convening information
- *disinformation*: the provision of misleading and alternative-deflecting information
- *over-information*: the provision of so much information that the relevant truth becomes indiscernible

The last of these is not insignificant. After all, a good way to conceal a needle is to build a haystack up around it. Burying a secret under a mountain of other information is a promising pathway to concealment.

When there is a breach in the wall of security with which confidential reports are generally surrounded, not only is the value of such reports annihilated but also collateral damage ramifies throughout the whole correlative reporting process. Thus, when the code used for a given message is broken, the whole region of its use is affected.

Accordingly, secrecy breeds secrecy. When X penetrates Y's secrets, it is generally critical for X to avert Y's realization of this fact, lest Y take suitable countermeasures. But if Y has indeed managed to penetrate X's penetrating, Y would naturally strive to avert X's being aware of these to facilitate further countermeasures. And this cycle has no automatic end. For better or worse, secrecy is self-potentiating.

The most highly security classified—and thereby most recipient-restricted—reports are those whose recipients are personally and individually named indicated in a prefix to the report. Next come those reports whose receipt is limited to those who work in a particular problem or project and who correspondingly have a "need to know" the content of that report. And then there follows increasingly larger groups to whose performance-mission the reported information has some—but increasingly allocated—degree of relevance.

This problem of information security and secrecy opens up a wide range of issues that need not be pursued for present purposes. Just one further point: Even the technically most superior means of protecting message security become vulnerable in the hands of incompetent or careless users.[11] And it can sometimes do an enemy favors. Early in the Second World War, to avoid compromising their own super-secret coding apparatus, the Allied cryptographers on occasion sent messages from one station to another encoded by the enemy's Enigma machine to which both stations had access.[12]

UTILIZATION URGENCY

Consideration urgency was already presented in chapter 4, but here it is urgency in implementing and utilization at issue. Reports that have a bearing on matters of action are generally time-sensitive. Their utility carries an expiration date and time is often of the essence. (There is generally no point in closing the barn door after the horse is gone.) The sooner the enemy's troop movements are reported, the more effectively a suitable response can be launched. Time and tide wait for no one, and if we are to implement reported information to good effect, we often have to be speedy about it. Often it is impossible to avoid the premature implementation of reports. Matters must often be resolved on the basis of incomplete and imperfect information. Amid the unstoppable folding of affairs, decisions cannot be postponed until all relevant reports are in.[13]

When the "use by" deadline lies in the very near future, the report deserves to be categorized as HIGHLY URGENT. In the Second World War the processing of intercepted messages at Bletchley Park, Britain's decoding center, was subject to a system of Z grading assigned to messages between one and five Z's ,depending on the appraised urgency of processing. The ZZZZZ items required not only the most immediate attention but also were presumably the most immediately actionable and significant.[14]

Strictly speaking, two sorts of things can be at issue with urgency. On the one hand there is the reactive urgency at issue with the conviction that *something be done about it* at the proper time (which may not lie in the immediate future). The idea here is that it is urgent (that is, essential that the report be acted on). On the other hand is the conviction that *something be done soon*—in the immediate future. This is the chronological urgency of response. Granted, the two will often—and perhaps even generally—coincide. We then have the situation reflected in Winston Churchill's famed annotation, "Action this day!"

It is often helpful for the reportee to give the reporter their best estimate of the urgency of a report. But this must be done with conservative care. The present-day practice of many advertisers to mark their postal communications with "Urgent, open at once!" often as not secures their missives an immediate transit into the wastebasket.

COST-BENEFIT MATTERS

Under-reporting can be a fatal flaw, depriving the reportee of much-needed information. But over-reporting has its negativities as well. The processing of reports imposes costs: it requires time, attention, effort, and so on to prepare, transmit, consider, evaluate, and utilize reports.

This means—among other things—that a report should not be overelaborate. Reportage (like entities) should not be multiplied beyond necessity like so much else; the management of reports is subject to the principle of rational conservation of effort. Reporting should avoid making needless demands on reporters and reportees alike.

Intelligent gathering in military and diplomatic contexts is accordingly subject to the decidedly vexing—and ironic—reality that here, as often elsewhere, there is an inverse relationship between quality and quantity. Low-grade information often comes in great floods, while high-grade information comes in small dribbles. And this can mean that the really significant messages are enveloped by the massive amounts of insignificant reportage. The background "noise" of mass reportage makes it hard to discern the occasional key signals.[15]

Actionable reports are the very crème de la crème of reportage. And the proper assessment of the action implications of reports is the most difficult and important thing that a recipient is called upon to do. Perplexity inevitably arises when a report whose truth is of dubious credential would—if correct—urgently require a significant response. Here, the risks run both ways, with action and inaction alike. No resolution of general principle is available with respect to such cases. What is needed here is good judgment and, perhaps no less importantly, good luck.

CONCLUSION

REPORTS DO NOT PROVIDE INFORMATION AS SUCH: what they provide is *purported* information whose correctness and utility is always up for consideration. We certainty cannot manage without reports, but managing with them can be a challenging business, requiring a machine with many different moving parts. So many diverse procedures are involved in productive report management and so many different contributions must be duly coordinated in the creation, transmission, interpretation, and implementation of reports that collaborative coordination across a wide spectrum of contributions becomes necessary. Effective reportage and its proper exploitation is a complex process that requires the smooth combination of many factors. By the purposive nature of the enterprise, it is a complex business. Various sorts of dedication and compatibility are called for along a long chain of diversified modes of operation. Particularly in matters of the state, the effective operation of this many linked chain requires a system of suitable and ingenious design. For the aim is not just to provide information but *useful* information, something that goes beyond the provider to bring the client into the picture as well. To understand the whole process adequately, one must be concerned with the reported message in its relation to its sources, its providers, its transmission, its reception, its appreciation, and its utilization. And at every step along this route there is a prospect of possible malfunction.

In dealing with reports it has to be borne in mind that our access to information is generally imperfect and incomplete. The evidentiation of a factual contention is never totally conclusive. Observational substantiation can leave us in the lurch. There is always the possibility of a slip between the cup and the lip. The entire process opens up scope not just for human error but for human malevolence as well. Even what looks, waddles, and quacks like a duck may in suitably inauspicious circumstances fail to be so; the dog that has often licked one's had may this time bite one's ankle. It is always appropriate to examine the credentials of a report.

Developments out of the ordinary course of things thereby tend to be out of the range of consideration by intelligence consumers. Regarding the Germany surprise parachute attack on Crete in 1941, one commentator remarks regarding Lieutenant General Bernard Freyberg, the British commander, that "No island has ever before been captured *except* from the sea. It was therefore natural for Freyberg to take the seashore threat seriously. Like every other historical event his decision can be fairly judged only in the light of the probable assumptions and through patterns of the time."[1] This judgment sounds reasonable and fair-minded. And yet at the same time, it should also be acknowledged that it is nevertheless a prime duty of intelligence management to transcend "the probable assumptions and thought patterns of the time"—to "think outside the box," as the popular expression has it.

Evaluating reports can be a complex business. There is an inevitable evidential gap between the supportive evidence we have and the objectively factual claims we base upon it. The information actually at our disposal in such matters substantiates and confirms our claims but does not altogether establish them. What it affords is not the categorical certainty of assured truth but some (at best high) degree of plausibility or probability.

And recent scholarship in matters of cognition and information theory often dwell on certain natural human shortcomings and deficiencies in the exploitation of information.[2] In one important report the present deliberations lends support to this point of view. For the study of intelligence reportage throws into sharp relief the phenomenon of what might be called normality tropism—the tendency to resist acknowledging exceptions to the rule at face value and to insist on dismissing seemingly extraordinary occurrences, in effect to reset low possibilities at zero. Even in the best of conditions, there is always some chance of error.

Unavoidably, we always run some risk in accepting and implementing a report. So at this point the general principles of risk management come into play. It becomes necessary to make a careful assessment of the nature and magnitude of the risks at issue. And it has to be borne in mind that risk taking is a two-way street. For there are risks of commission and omission, of misaction and inaction. And the stakes can run from the merely cognitive (being wrong) to the actually catastrophic. When one accepts and, above all, implements reports, the associated risks must always be weighted with due care. Even as the eliminability of physical friction precludes the realization of a perfectly efficient machine, so the eliminability of cognitive friction means that there can be no perfectly efficient reportage. Categorical certainty is a mirage in matters of reporting. Success can be misled, transmissions corrupted, interpretations erroneous, implementations mismanaged. In communicative as in moral life, perfection is inaccessible to mere mortals. All one can ask for is that those concerned take do care to achieve the achievable.

The reporter must be mindful of the needs of the recipient: of what now can and should be done in the light of the reported information. And the recipient must be mindful of the situation of the reporter: of the reporter's strengths and weaknesses in relation to securing desired information. In consequence, empathy is a crucial asset in report management. The provider of a report does well to imagine themself in the shoes of its recipient, asking "What sort of information on this topic does the recipient need or want to have, how does he or she propose to use it, and just what will he or she make of the material I am providing?" And analogously, the recipient does well to think of the provider's position, asking "Does the reporter really understand what it is that I need, and to what extent is he or she in a position actually to supply it?" Where two positions are collaborating in digging a tunnel through a mountain from opposite sides, they do well to ensure that they will meet in the middle.

It bears repeating that intelligence reportage is an enterprise whose proper conduct requires the collaborative coordination of many individuals and their various functions. Source management, reporting arrangements, and the subsequent processes of transmission, interpretation, and utilization must all mesh smoothly like a very complex machine, and this is spectacularly true in military and diplomatic affairs. Unless all its parts are interlinked with observation, reportage, transmission, reception, interpretation, and implantation functionally coordinated into one reciprocally coordinated whole, with each component's duty geared to its neighbors', the definitive aims of the overall enterprise cannot be realized.

No single consideration is more critical in this connection than the need for systemic integration through functionally effective coordination among the constituted elements of the entire process. Intelligently operated intelligence reportage must operate on holistic principles. The management of intelligence information can only achieve its maximum effectiveness where there is a system that conjoins all its various components in a network of mutually supportive feedback loops, where overall the functioning of each supports and is supported by that of the others.

Despite the tendency to think that the system needs to be the structure of a pyramidal hierarchy with a single directive potential at the top, this is not the right picture. Rather, like a hospital, an ant colony, or for that matter a human brain, the best organization should be a spider web–like constructible of local connections enlightened into a productively functioning whole. Granted there has to be externally managed quality control, however, the issue is ultimately the effective functioning of the organic system as a whole—doing the job that evolution does with respect to actual organisms. And there have to be system antitheses to devise ways of fixing discernible malfunctions. In short, there has to be control of the system's modus operandi. But this need not and almost certainly should not come from within the system itself. And there are many good reasons for this—above all the self-serving inertia of any bureaucracy. And so there should in the end be a division of labor.

The quality control of the particular products of an intelligence management system should be left to the system itself, but the quality control of the overall performance of the system (its modus operandi, if you will) should come from without via the system external clients who put those products to work. In this regard then, there is a hierarchy of control. But such a hierarchy of supervision need not—and indeed should not—be implemented within the design of the system by which the constitution of intelligence is managed, a design whose nonhierarchic organic structure should ideally reflect the organic interlinkage of the processes involved.

An intelligence system is—or should be—analogous to a complex mechanism designed to function well with respect to general principles of purposive efficacy. But once this desideratum is achieved, the mechanism should be allowed to do its work undisturbed, accepting its products exactly because they issue from the functioning of a well-designed system. "Don't second guess the experts" should be a governing maxim here.

NOTES

CHAPTER 1. REPORTS AND OUR NEED FOR INFORMATION

1. See Wolfgang Riepl, *Das Nachrichtenwesen des Altertums, mit besonderer Rücksicht auf die Römer* (Leipzig: B. G. Teubner, 1913).

2. David Alvarez, *Secret Messages: Codebreaking and American Diplomacy* (Lawrence, KS: University Press of Kansas, 2000), 204–5.

3. The obvious exception here is when many consilient ones are provided independently.

4. On this issue, see R. A. Ratcliffe, *Delusions of Intelligence: Enigma, Ultra, and the End of Secure Ciphers* (Cambridge: Cambridge University Press, 2006).

5. For interesting examples, see Ronald Lewin, *Ultra Goes to War: The First Account of World War II's Greatest Secret Based on Official Documents* (New York: McGraw-Hill 1978).

6. Quoted in John W. Leeter-Bennett, ed., *Action This Day: Working with Churchill* (New York: St. Martin's Press, 1969), 20.

7. Hugh Trevor-Roper, *The Philby Affair* (London: William Kimber, 1968), 67.

8. One very important item missed altogether in Allied signals monitoring was Hitler's order canceling operation "Sea Lion," the projected invasion of Britain. See Wilhelm Agrell and Bo Huldt, *Clio Goes Spying: Eight Essays on the History of Intelligence* (Stockholm: Lundt University Press, 1983).

9. For details of this aspect, see Ewen Montagu, *The Man Who Never Was* (Philadelphia: Lippincott, 1954).

CHAPTER 2. REPORTING AND ITS SOURCES

1. See F. C. Bartlett, *Remembering: A Study in Experimental and Social Psychology* (Cambridge: Cambridge University Press, 1932).

2. Ralph Bennett, *Behind the Battle* (London: Pimlico, 1999), 315. Good faith is of course a pivotal consideration. The extraordinary attention of espionage agencies to the knowledge-ability of their reporters, not their ideological relativity, is illustrated time and again in Nigel West and Oleg Tsarer, *The Crown Jewels: British Secretes at the Heart of the KGB Archives* (New Haven: Yale University Press, 1999).

3. Anthony C. Brown, *Bodyguard of Lies* (New York: Harper & Row, 1975), 816.

4. See for example, Tony Mathews, *Shadows Dancing: Japan's Espionage against the West* (London: Robert Hale, 1993), 183.

5. On these issues, consider the interesting examples of reportage malfunction described in chapter 10 of Anthony C. Brown, *Bodyguard of Lies* (New York: Harper & Row, 1975), 551–64.

6. Kenneth Strong, *Men of Intelligence* (London, Cassell, 1970), 28.

7. See Carl Boyd, *Hitler's Japanese Confidant: General Ōshima Hiroshi and MAGIC Intelligence* (Lawrence, KS: University Press of Kansas, 1993).

8. Usefully relevant considerations can be found in David Lewis, *Convention: A Philosophical Study* (Cambridge MA: Harvard University Press, 1969). But contrast Angus Ross, "Why Do We Believe What We are Told?" *Ratio* 28 (1986): 69–88.

9. On these issues, see the Nicholas Rescher, *Presumption and the Practice of Tentative Cognition* (Cambridge: Cambridge University Press, 2006).

10. See, for example, J. G. Blight and D. A. Welch, *Intelligence and the Cuban Missile Crisis* (London: Frank Cass, 1998). 45.

CHAPTER 3. CONTENT MATTERS

1. See Roberta Wohlstetter, *Pearl Harbor: Warning and Decision* (Stanford, CA: Stanford University Press, 1962).

2. Aristotle, *Nicomachaen Ethics*, 1094a12–23. It is to Aristotle's credit that (as the *Index Aristoleticus* of Bonitz indicates) he devotes almost as much attention to precision (akraveia etc.) as to truth (*alêstheine*, etc.).

3. On these issues, again see Roberta Wohlstetter, *Pearl Harbor: Warning and Decision* (Stanford, CA: Stanford University Press, 1962).

4. See Jürgen Rohwer, "Radio Intelligence in the Battle of the Atlantic," in *Clio Goes Spying: Eight Essays on the History of Intelligence,* edited by Wilhelm Agrell and Bo Huldt (Stockholm: Laundt University Publishers, 1983), 85–107.

5. Christopher M. Andrew and Vasili Mitrokhin, *The Sword and the Shield: The Mitrokhin Archive and the Secret History of the KGB* (New York: Basic Books, 1999).

6. The Germans did much the same with British agents in the Netherlands.

7. Wohlstetter, *Pearl Harbor*

8. P. S. de Laplace, *A Philosophical Essay on Probabilities,* edited by F. W. Truscott and F. L. Emory (New York, 1951), chap. 11,109–25 (see esp. 120–22).

9. See Heinz Bonatz, *Seekrieg im Aether* (Herford: Mittler, 1981).

CHAPTER 4. TRANSMISSION

1. See Wolfgang Riepl, *Das Nachrichtenwesen des Altertums, mit besonderer Rücksicht auf die Römer* (Leipzig: B.G. Teubner, 1913).

2. See Roberta Wohlstetter, *Pearl Harbor: Warning and Decision* (Stanford, CA: Stanford University Press, 1962).

3. R. A. Ratcliffe, *Delusions of Intelligence: Enigma, Ultra, and the End of Secure Ciphers* (Cambridge: Cambridge University Press, 2006), 44–45.

4. The time delays required for description often renders information access useless. See, for example, Bradley F. Smith, *The Ultra-Magic Deals and the Most Secret Special Relationship, 1940–1946* (Novato, CA: Presidio, 1992).

5. Ratcliffe, *Delusions of Intelligence*, 44.

6. On this issue, see Allen Dulles, *The Secret Surrender* (New York: Harper & Row, 1966), esp. 255–56.

7. See Wohlstetter, *Pearl Harbor*; and Gordon W. Prange, *At Dawn We Slept: The Untold Story of Pearl Harbor* (New York: McGraw-Hill, 1981).

8. For details see Robert Butow, *Japan's Decision to Surrender* (Stanford: Stanford University Press, 1954), chap. 9.

9. Butow, *Japan's Decision to Surrender*, chap. 10.

10. A highly interesting instance of reports much too late for effective reaction, albeit nevertheless of substantive historical interest, is the Signal Intelligence Service's (SIS), which later became the National Security Agency (NSA), Venona project based on the long after-the-fact decryption of Soviet communications of espionage matters in the United States during the Second World War. For details, see J. E. Haynes and Harvey Klehr, *Venona: Decoding Soviet Espionage in America* (New Haven, CT: Yale University Press, 1999).

11. Quoted in Ralph Bennett, *Behind the Battle* (London: Pimlico, 1999), xxi.

12. See Wohlstetter, *Pearl Harbor*.

13. For details, see Butow, *Japan's Decision to Surrender*.

14. See Richard Rhodes, *Dark Sun: The Making of the Hydrogen Bomb* (New York: Simon & Schuster, 1995).

CHAPTER 5. RECEPTION

1. Usefully relevant discussions can be found in David Lewis, *Convention: A Philosophical Study* (Cambridge: Harvard University Press, 1969). But also compare with Angus Ross, "Why Do We Believe What We Are Told," *Ratio* 28 (1986): 69–88.

2. See John Lewis Gaddis, *George F. Kennan: An American Life* (New York: Penguin, 2011).

3. Anne Armstrong, *Unconditional Surrender: The Impact of the Casablanca Policy upon World War II* (New Brunswick: Rutgers University Press, 1961), 252.

4. On Stalin's unwillingness to heed the numerous reports of projected German action against the USSR, see Ralph Bennett, *Behind the Battle* (London: Pimlico, 1999), 92–93.

5. Charles Whiting, *Hitler's Secret War* (London: Leo Cooper, 2000), 153.

6. On the complex relations that sometimes exist between the security services of a country and its political leadership, see Ian Colvin, *Chief of Intelligence: Admiral Wilhelm Canaris* (London: Gollancz, 1951).

7. For various illustrations of this circumstance, see David Alvarez, *Secret Messages: Codebreaking and American Diplomacy* (Lawrence, KS: University Press of Kansas, 2000).

8. On these issues, see Edward Regis, ed., *Extraterrestrials* (Cambridge: Cambridge University Press, 1985).

9. See Carl Boyd, *Hitler's Japanese Confidant: General Ōshima Hiroshi and MAGIC Intelligence* (Lawrence, KS: University Press of Kansas, 1993).

10. On the Dieppe Raid, see John Hughes-Wilson, *Military Intelligence Blunders and Cover-ups* (Bath: Robinson, 2004); as well as Anthony C. Brown, *Bodyguard of Lies* (New York: Harper and Row, 1975), 84–87. See also See Gert Buchheit, *Der deutsche Geheimdienst* (München: Paul List Verlag, 1967), 340–41.

11. To be sure, the Germans having broken Japan's diplomatic codes had left little doubt on the matter. Keeping secrets from one's allies was not a Japanese monopoly.

12. See, for example, David Alvarez, *Allied and Axis Signals Intelligence in World War II* (London: Frank Cass, 1999), 78–81; and also R. A. Ratcliffe, *Delusions of Intelligence: Enigma, Ultra, and the End of Secure Ciphers* (Cambridge: Cambridge University Press, 2006), 162–63.

13. Alvarez, *Secret Messages*, 232–322.

14. Quoted in Harvey A. Deweerd, "Strategic Surprise in the Korean War," *Orbis* 6, no. 3 (1962): 451.

15. See David Kahn, *Hitler's Spies* (New York: Macmillan, 1978), 539.

16. Kahn, *Hitler's Spies*, 540.

17. Edward Bridges in John Wheeler-Bennett, ed., *Action This Day* (New York: St. Martin's, 1969), 228.

18. Alvarez, *Secret Messages*, 57–58, 242–43.

19. Alvarez, *Secret Messages*, 242.

20. For detailed evidence of Hitler's micromanagement, see D. M. Glantz, ed., *Hitler and His Generals: Military Conference, 1942–1945* (New York: Eugene Books, 2003).

21. See Wilhelm von Schramm, *Verrat im Zweiten Weiten: Vom Kampf der Geheimdienste in Europa, Berichte und Dokumentation* (Dusseldorf, 1967), 276. Hitler denounced a well-informed and accurate report on Soviet troop activities as "complete idiocy" and annotated a report on society agriculture with the notation "This cannot be!" See Joseph E. Persico, *Roosevelt's Secret War* (New York: Random House, 2001), 451.

22. For multiple attestations to Churchill's regard for intelligence and concern with its details, see Brown, *Bodyguard of Lies*.

CHAPTER 6. COGNITIVE IMPORTANCE

1. On the wide-ranging significance of signals intelligence, see David Alvarez, *Secret Messages: Codebreaking and American Diplomacy* (Lawrence, KS: University Press of Kansas, 2000).

2. What Shakespeare said of worth in general certainly holds for cognitive worth or importance: "But value dwells not in particular will; / It holds his estimate and dignity / As well wherein 'tis precious of itself / As in the prizer" (*Troilus and Cressida*, act 2, sc. 2, lines 53–56).

3. On these matters, see the Nicholas Rescher, *Epistemetrics* (Cambridge: Cambridge University Press, 2006).

4. Larry Laudan is one of the few writers on the philosophy of science who recognize that, since the answering of important questions and the resolution of important problems is the object of the scientific enterprise, an adequate theory of science must address the issue of importance. Unfortunately, however, he speaks of "interesting questions [or] in other words . . . important problems" (Larry Laudan, *Progress and Its Problems* [Berkeley: University of California Press, 1977], 13). And this is highly problematic. In science as elsewhere, issues can be interesting without necessarily thereby being very important.

CHAPTER 7. INTERPRETATION PROBLEMS

1. Kenneth Strong, *Men of Intelligence* (London, Cassell, 1970), 140.

2. On these issues see Stephen Budaowsky, *Code Warriors* (New York: Alfred A. Knopf, 2016).

3. Ralph Bennett, *Behind the Battle* (London: Pimlico, 1999), p. 309.

4. Ralph Bennett, *Behind the Battle* (London: Pimlico, 1999), 309.

5. See, for example, J. G. Blight and D. A. Welch, *Intelligence and the Cuban Missile Crisis* (London: Frank Cass, 1998), 207.

6. This abstract approach to the matter is not entirely fictitious. Prior to the attack at Pearl Harbor, Japan's agents in Honolulu were provided with a grand system covering the harbor and requested to go to suitable observation points to locate ships anchorages. The absence of the American carriers proved to be the operation's fatal flaw. On these matters, see Gordon W. Prange, *At Dawn We Slept: The Untold Story of Pearl Harbor* (New York: McGraw-Hill, 1981).

7. There are innumerable illustrations of this circumstance. For one particularly vivid example, see Wilhelm Agrell and Bo Huldt, *Clio Goes Spying: Eight Essays on the History of Intelligence* (Stockholm: Landt University Publishers, 1983), 184.

8. Bennett, *Behind the Battle*, 309.

9. For a vivid illustration of the need of context in report interpretation, see J. P. M. Showell, *German Naval Code Breakers* (Annapolis, MD: Naval Institute Press, 2003), 48.

10. On these issues, see especially the discussion in Robin W. Winks's *Cloak and Gown: Scholars in the Secret War, 1939–1961* (New Haven: Yale University Press, 1987), with its sagacious concern for the interaction between intelligence interpretative and historiographical method.

11. David Kahn, *Hitler's Spies* (New York: Macmillan, 1978), 532.

12. For details regarding this episode, see Prange, *At Dawn We Slept*.

13. Carl von Clausewitz, *On War*, trans. J. J. Graham (New York: Barnes & Noble, 1966), appendix 4, "On Principles."

14. John Hughes-Wilson, *Military Intelligence Blunders* (New York: Carroll & Graf, 1999), 211; compare the plaint that in the Gulf War of 1990–1991 "there was simply *too much* intelligence" (Hughes-Wilson, *Military Intelligence Blunders*, 345).

15. Hughes-Wilson, *Military Intelligence Blunders*, 357.

16. Roberta Wohlstetter, *Pearl Harbor: Warning and Decision* (Stanford: Stanford University Press, 1962).

17. Wohlstetter, *Pearl Harbor*, 180.

18. The pioneer here was Leon Festinger, whose *A Theory of Cognitive Dissonance* (Stanford: Stanford University Press, 1957) remains a classic in the field.

19. On the specifics, see R. A. Ratcliffe, *Delusions of Intelligence: Enigma, Ultra, and the End of Secure Ciphers* (Cambridge: Cambridge University Press, 2006), especially chapter 3.

20. On these issues, see Richard Langhorne and Francis H. Hinsley, *Diplomacy and Intelligence during the Second World War* (Cambridge: Cambridge University Press, 1985).

21. See Anne Armstrong, *Unconditional Surrender: The Impact of the Casablanca Policy upon World War II* (New Brunswick: Rutgers University Press, 1961), 250.

22. The Delphi method was developed in the 1950s by Olaf Helmer and two collaborators in the Mathematics Division of the RAND Corporation, Norman Dalkey and the present author. (All three of us held PhDs in philosophy, which may have increased our sympathy for eccentric approaches.) The method drew inspiration from the study by Abraham Kaplan, A. L. Skogstad, and M. A. Girshik, "The Prediction of Social and Technological Events," *Public Opinion Quarterly* 14 (1950): 93–110. It was initially explained in Olaf Helmer and Nicholas Rescher, "On the Epistemology of the Inexact Sciences," *Management Science* 6 (1959): 25–52. (This article reprints an internal RAND Corporation paper of 1958 and was the earliest discussion on Delphi published in the open literature.) For other descriptions, see Olaf Helmer's *Social Technology* (New York: Basic, 1961), and his *Looking Forward: A Guide to Future's Research* (Beverly Hills: Sage, 1983). For further references, see Roger M. Cooke, *Experts in Uncertainty: Opinion and Subjective Probability in Science* (New York: Oxford University Press, 1991), 299 and throughout, especially chapter 11, "Combining Expert Opinion." Good discussions of Delphi are also found in Harold A. Linstone and Murray Turoff, eds., *The Delphi Method: Techniques and Applications* (Reading MA: Addison Wesley, 1975); and in Joseph P. Martino, *Technological Forecasting for Decisionmaking* (New York: American Elzevier, 1972), 28–64. Beyond these classics, there are also numerous more recent studies on the Delphi method.

CHAPTER 8. EVALUATION

1. See, for example, the description of the NSA's position during the Hungary/Suez crisis of 1956 as reported in Stephen Budaowsky, *Code Warriors* (New York: Alfred Knopf, 2016), 205–6, 307–8.

2. Consider an analogy: In tossing a die, it is unlikely that a 6 ("the right answer") will result. But with five tosses the chances of at least one 6 are very good.

3. Patrick Beesly, *Very Special Admiral: The Life of Admiral J. H. Godfrey* (London: Hamist Hamilton, 1980), 186–87.

4. And it is interesting to note in this regard that in the Second World War, Admiral Alan G. Kirk, the director of naval intelligence issued a circular requiring the retaining of the sources of intelligence reports issued by his department, ranging from *A* for unimpeachable reliability to *D* for questionable information, only usable in the context of confirming otherwise available reportage. See J. M Dorwart, *Conflict of Duty* (Annapolis: Naval Institute Press, 1983), 156–57.

5. Note, however, that this particular arithmetization treats reliability and plausibility as equisignificant. If one of them were to be given greater weight, the formula would have to be complicated. For example, by using $\sqrt{R} \times P$ instead of $R \times P$ as measure, we would ensure giving greater weight to content plausibility (P) as against source reliability (R).

6. In the Second World War the British intelligence agencies used a Z-allocation scheme to indicate urgency, ranging from a single Z to reflect low priorities to a five Z assignment of reports of imperative urgency. See Nigel West, *GCHQ: The Secret Wireless War: 1900–1986* (London: Weidenfeld & Nicholson, 1986), 178.

7. Further complications arise when reports of different merit are combined as premises to derive a conclusion. One sensible approach would then be to adopt the classic weakest link principle, which assigns to the conclusion the status of the weakest premise. On these issues, see the author's *Plausible Reasoning* (Amsterdam: Van Gorcum, 1976).

8. On these issues, see Peter Gärdenfors, *Knowledge in Flux: Modelling the Dynamics of Epistemic State* (Cambridge, MA: MIT Press, 1988); and Gilbert Harmon, *Change in View* (Cambridge MA: MIT Press, 1986).

CHAPTER 9. UTILIZATION

1. Bradley F. Smith, *The Ultra-Magic Deals and the Most Secret Special Relationship, 1940–1946* (Novato, California: Presidio, 1992).

2. On Mill see Alan Ryan, *John Stuart Mill* (New York, Pantheon Books, 1970).

3. See, for example, Henry C. Clausen and Bruce Lee, *Pearl Harbor: Final Judgment* (New York: Crown Publishers, 1992), 295.

4. The individual informed by an informer (or informant) is of course an informee, although the English language somehow fails to acknowledge this.

5. For details, see D. C. James, *The Years of MacArthur*, vol. 2 (Boston: Houghton Mifflin, 1975), 3–15.

6. For various illustration of this situation, see R. A. Ratcliffe, *Delusions of Intelligence: Enigma, Ultra, and the End of Secure Ciphers* (Cambridge: Cambridge University Press, 2006).

7. This was Hitler's personal order ("Fuehrerbefehl") of January 11, 1940. See Gert Buchheit, *Der deutsche Geheimdienst* (München: Paul List Verlag, 1967); and also David Kahn, *Hitler's Spies* (New York: Macmillan, 1978).

8. Like any instrument, secrecy is subject both to use and abuse. Sissela Bok's *Secrets* (New York: Pantheon Books, 1983) is rather tendentiously focused on the negative side.

9. For a detailed account of Churchill's Coventry dilemma, see A. C. Brown, *Bodyguard of Lies* (New York: Harper & Row, 1975), 40–47.

10. David Alvarez, *Allied and Axis Signals Intelligence in World War II* (London: Frank Cass, 1999).

11. For numerous illustrations of this fact that no system is proof against human incompetence, see Stephen Budianski, *Battle of Wits: The Complete Story of Codebreaking in World War II* (New York: Free Press, 2000).

12. See Budianski, *Battle of Wits*, 134. See also Ronald Lewin, *Ultra Goes to War: The First Account of World War II's Greatest Secret Based on Official Documents* (New York, Mc-Graw-Hill 1978), 62, 124.

13. See, for example, Togo Shigenori, *The Cause of Japan* (New York: Simon and Schuster, 1956).

14. See Thomas Parrish, *The Ultra Americans* (New York: Stein and Day, 1986), 139.

15. For a vivid illustration of this phenomenon, see Roberta Wohlstetter, *Pearl Harbor: Warning and Decision* (Stanford, CA: Stanford University Press, 1962).

CONCLUSION

1. Ralph Bennett, *Behind the Battle* (London: Random House, 1999), 295.

2. See in particular Leon Festinger, *A Theory of Cognitive Dissonance* (Stanford Stanford University Press, 1957); and Daniel Kahneman, Paul Slovic, and Amos Tversky, *Judgment under Uncertainty* (New York: Cambridge University Press, 1982).

SELECTED BIBLIOGRAPHY

The focus of this book has been on reportage in matters of state, involving primarily diplomacy and warfare. There are but few books that deal with these issues at a level of systematic generality. Instructive glimpses are afforded in the following sources:

Beesly, Patrick. *Very Special Admiral: The Life of Admiral J. H. Godfrey.* London: Hamish Hamilton, 1980.

Beesly, Patrick. *Very Special Intelligence: The Story of Admiralty's Operational Intelligence Centre, 1939–1945.* London: Hamish Hamilton, 1977.

Bennett, Ralph. *Behind the Battle: Intelligence in the War with Germany, 1939–1945.* London: Pimlico, 1999.

Dulles, Allen. *The Craft of Intelligence.* New York: Harper & Row, 1963.

Wohlstetter, Roberta. *Pearl Harbor: Warning and Decision.* Stanford, CA: Stanford University Press, 1962.

Moreover, what follows are two classic works bearing on purely theoretical issues regarding the use of reports in situations of incomplete information.

Festinger, Leon. *A Theory of Cognitive Dissonance.* Stanford, CA: Stanford University Press, 1957.

Kahneman, Daniel, Paul Slovic, and Amos Tversky, *Judgment under Uncertainty.* New York: Cambridge University Press, 1982.

Other works that have informed the present deliberations include the following.

Agrell, Wilhelm, and Bo Huldt, eds. *Clio Goes Spying: Eight Essays on the History of Intelligence.* Stockholm: Landt University Publishers, 1983.

Alvarez, David. *Allied and Axis Signals Intelligence in World War II.* London: Frank Cass, 1999.

Alvarez, David. *Secret Messages: Codebreaking and American Diplomacy.* Lawrence, KS: University Press of Kansas, 2000.

Andrew, Christopher M., and Vasili Mitrokhin. *The Sword and the Shield: The Mitrokhin Archive and the Secret History of the KGB.* New York: Basic, 1999.

Aristotle. *The Nicomachaen Ethics.* Translated by W. D. Ross. New York: Oxford University Press, 1983.

Armstrong, Anne. *Unconditional Surrender: The Impact of the Casablanca Policy upon World War II.* New Brunswick: Rutgers University Press, 1961.

Banford, James. *The Puzzle Palace.* New York: Houghton Mifflin Harcourt, 1983.

Bartlett, F. C. *Remembering: A Study of Experimental and Social Psychology.* Cambridge: Cambridge University Press, 1932.

Bauer, Ludwig. *Decrypted Secrets.* 4th ed. Berlin: Springer, 2007.

Blight James G., and David A Welch, eds. *Intelligence and the Cuban Missile Crisis.* London: Frank Cass, 1998.

Bok, Sissela. *Secrets: On the Ethics of Concealment and Revelation.* New York: Pantheon Books, 1983.

Boyd, Carl. *Hitler's Japanese Confidant: General Ōshima Hiroshi and MAGIC Intelligence.* Lawrence, KS: University Press of Kansas, 1993.

Brown, Anthony C. *Bodyguard of Lies.* New York: Harper & Row, 1975.

Buchheit, Gert. *Der deutsche Geheimdienst.* München: Paul List Verlag, 1967.

Butow, Robert. *Japan's Decision to Surrender.* Stanford, CA: Stanford University Press, 1954.

Clausen, Henry C., and Bruce Lee. *Pearl Harbor: Final Judgment.* New York: Crown Publishers, 1992.

Colvin, Ian. *Chief of Intelligence: Admiral Wilhelm Canaris.* London: Gollancz, 1951.

Dorwart, J. M. *Conflict of Duty.* Annapolis: Naval Institute Press, 1983.

Dulles, Allen. *The Secret Surrender.* New York: Harper & Row, 1966.

Gaddis, John Lewis. *George F. Kennan: An American Life.* New York: Penguin, 2011.

Glantz, D. M., ed. *Hitler and His Generals: Military Conferences, 1942–1945.* New York: Eugene, 2003.

Haynes, J. E., and Harvey Klehr. *Venona: Decoding Soviet Espionage in America.* New Haven: Yale University Press, 1999.

Hughes-Wilson, John. *Military Intelligence Blunders and Cover-Ups.* Bath: Robinson, 2004.

Jones, R. V. *Most Secret War: British Scientific Intelligence, 1939–1945.* London: Hamish Hamilton, 1978.

Jörgensen, Christer. *Hitler's Espionage Machine: German Intelligence Agencies and Operations during World War II.* Staplehurst, UK: Spellmount, 2004.

Kahn, David. *Hitler's Spies.* New York: Macmillan, 1978.

Langhorne, Richard, and Francis H. Hinsley. *Diplomacy and Intelligence during the Second World War.* Cambridge: Cambridge University Press, 1985.

Laplace, Pierre Simon, marquis de. *A Philosophical Essay on Probabilities.* Edited by F. W. Truscott and F. L. Emory. New York: Dover, 1951.

Lewin, Ronald. *The American Magic: Codes, Ciphers, and the Defeat of Japan.* New York: Farrar Straus Giroux, 1982.

Lewin, Ronald. *Ultra Goes to War: The First Account of World War II's Greatest Secret Based on Official Documents.* New York: McGraw-Hill, 1978.

Lewis, David. *Convention: A Philosophical Study.* Cambridge: Harvard University Press, 1969.

Matthews, Tony. *Shadows Dancing: Japan's Espionage against the West.* London: Robert Hale, 1993.

Montagu, Ewen. *The Man Who Never Was.* Philadelphia: Lippincott, 1954.

Normanbrook, Norman Brook, Baron. *Action This Day: Working with Churchill.* Edited by John Wheeler-Bennett. New York: St. Martin's Press, 1969.

Persico, Joseph E. *Roosevelt's Secret War.* New York: Random House, 2001.

Prange, Gordon W. *At Dawn We Slept: The Untold Story of Pearl Harbor.* New York: McGraw-Hill, 1981.

Ratcliffe, R. A. *Delusions of Intelligence: Enigma, Ultra, and the End of Secure Ciphers.* Cambridge: Cambridge University Press, 2006.

Regis, Edward, ed. *Extraterrestrials: Science and Alien Intelligence.* Cambridge: Cambridge University Press, 1985.

Rescher, Nicholas. *Presumptions and the Practice of Tentative Cognition.* Cambridge: Cambridge University Press, 2006.

Riepl, Wolfgang. *Das Nachrichtenwesen des Altertums, mit besonderer Rücksicht auf die Römer.* Leipzig: B.G. Teubner, 1913.

Rohwer, Jürgen. "Radio Intelligence in the Battle of the Atlantic." In Agrell and Huldt, *Clio Goes Spying,* 85–107.

Ross, Angus. "Why Do We Believe What We Are Told?" *Ratio* 28 (1986): 69–88.

Schramms, Wilhelm von. *Verrat im zweiten Weltkreig.* 2nd ed. Düsseldorff: Econ Verlag, 1967.

Smith, Bradley F. *The Ultra-Magic Deals and the Most Secret Special Relationship, 1940–1946.* Novato, CA: Presidio, 1992.

Showell, J. P. M. *German Naval Code Breakers.* Annapolis, MD: Naval Institute Press, 2003.

Shigenori, Togo. *The Cause of Japan.* New York: Simon and Schuster, 1956.

Strong, Kenneth. *Men of Intelligence.* London: Cassell, 1970.

Trundle, Christopher N. *The Philosophy of Argument and Audience Reception.* Cambridge: Cambridge University Press, 2015.

West, Nigel. *GCHQ: The Secret Wireless War, 1900–86.* London: Weidenfeld & Nicholson, 1986.

West, Nigel, and Oleg Tsarer. *The Crown Jewels: British Secretes at the Heart of the KGB Archives.* New Haven: Yale University Press, 1999.

Whiting, Charles. *Hitler's Secret War.* London: Leo Cooper, 2000.

Winks, Robin W. *Cloak and Gown: Scholars on the Secret War, 1939–1961.* New York: William Morrow, 1987.

INDEX OF NAMES

Canaris, Wilhelm, 150
Cato, 32
Chiang, Kai-shek, 50
Churchill, Winston, 15,
    87–90, 110, 122, 136, 150,
    166n22(c5), 170n9(c9)
Clausen, Henry C., 169n3(c9)
Clausewitz, Carl von, 11, 109,
    167n13(c7)
Colvin, Ian, 165n6(c5)
Cooke, Roger M., 168n22(c7)
Croesus, 46

Dalkey, Norman, 168n22(c7)
Darlan, Jean Louis Xavier
    François, 64
Deweerd, Harvey A.,
    166n14(c5)
Dönitz, Karl, 14, 52, 56
Dorwart, J. M, 169n4(c8)
Dulles, Allen, 165n6(c4)

Festinger, Leon, 168n18(c7),
    170n2(con.)

Forbes, C. M., 141
Freyberg, Bernard, 158
Fuchs, Klaus, 30

Gaddis, John Lewis, 165n2(c5)
Gärdenfors, Peter, 169n8(c8)
Gehlen, Reinhard, 88
Girshik, M. A., 168n22(c7)
Godfrey, J. H., 130–33, 135,
    141
Grey, Charles, 141

Harmon, Gilbert, 169n8(c8)
Haynes, J. E., 165n10(c4)
Helmer, Olaf, 168n22(c7)
Herodotus, 46
Hess, Rudolf, 28
Hinsley, Francis H.,
    168n20(c7)
Hiss, Alger, 32, 39
Hitler, Adolf, 51, 79,
    87–90, 110, 150, 163n8(c1),
    166n20(c5), 166n21(c5),
    170n7(c9)

Hughes-Wilson, John,
166n10(c5), 168nn14–15(c7)
Huldt, Bo, 163n8(c1), 167n7(c7)
Hume, David, 54–55

Jackson, Andrew, 52
James, D. C., 169n5(c9)
James, William, 9
Johnson, Samuel, 19
Jones, R. V., 173

Kahn, David, 166n15(c5),
166n16(c5), 167n11(c7),
170n7(c9)
Kahneman, Daniel,
170n2(con.)
Kaplan, Abraham, 168n22(c7)
Kennan, George, 75
Kennedy, John F., 5
Kirk, Alan G., 169n4(c8)
Klehr, Harvey, 165n10(c4)

Langhorne, Richard,
168n20(c7)

Laplace, Pierre Simon,
marquis de, 54–55,
164n8(c3)
Laudan, Larry, 167n4(c6)
Lee, Bruce, 169n3(c9)
Lewin, Ronald, 163n5(c1),
170n12(c9)
Lewis, David, 164n8(c2),
165n1(c5)
Locke, John, 110

MacArthur, Douglas, 87,
147
Marco Polo, 6
Martino, Joseph P.,
168n22(c7)
Mathews, Tony, 613n4(c2)
McAuliffe, Anthony, 70
Menzies, Stewart, 28
Mill, John Stuart 141,
169n2(c9)
Mitrokhin, Vasili, 164n5(c3)
Montagu, Ewen, 163n9(c1)

Norwood, Melita S., 62

Ōshima, Hiroshi, 34, 80

Parrish, Thomas, 170n14(c9)
Patton, George S., 44, 82
Persico, Joseph E., 166n21(c5)
Philby, Kim, 150
Prange, Gordon W., 167n6(c7),
    167n12(c7)

Ratcliffe, R. A., 163n4(c1),
    164n3(c4), 165n5(c4),
    166n12(c5), 166n13(c5),
    168n19(c7), 169n6(c9)
Rhodes, Richard, 165n14(c4)
Riepl, Wolfgang, 163n1(c1),
    164n1(c4)
Rohwer, Jürgen, 164n4(c3)
Roosevelt, Franklin D., 40, 75,
    87–90
Ross, Angus, 164n8(c2),
    165n1(c5)
Ryan, Alan, 169n2(c9)

Schramm, Wilhelm von,
    166n21(c5)
Seifert, Walther, 87
Shakespeare, 166n2(c6)
Shannon, Claude, 115
Shigenori, Togo, 160n13(c9)
Showell, J. P. M. 167n9(c7)
Skogstad, A. L., 168n22(c7)
Slovic, Paul, 170n2(con.)
Smith, Bradley F., 165n4(c4),
    169n1(c9)
Sorge, Richard, 39, 49, 122
Stalin, Joseph, 12, 49, 51–52,
    67, 75, 90, 110, 121–22,
    165n4(c5)
Strong, Kenneth, 164n6(c2),
    167n1(c7)

Tayllerand, Charles Maurice
    de, 59
Temple, Henry John, 3rd
    Viscount Palmerston, 60
Tolstoy, Leo, 6
Trevor-Roper, Hugh 163n7(c1)

Truman, Harry S., 52
Tversky, Amos, 170n2(con.)
Twain, Mark, 25

von Paulus, Friedrich, 86
von Stauffenberg, Claus, 79

Welch, D. A., 164n10(c2),
    167n5(c7)
West, Nigel, 163n2(c2),
    169n6(c8)
Whiting, Charles, 165n5(c5)
Winks, Robin W., 167n10(c7)
Wohlstetter, Roberta,114–15,
    164n1(c3), 164n3(c3),
    164n3(c4), 164n7(c3),
    165n7(c4), 165n12(c4),
    168n16(c7), 168n17(c7),
    170n15(c9)